Natalie Portman's

Stark Reality

OTHER BOOKS BY JAMES L. DICKERSON

Nicole Kidman
A Kind of Life

Sons Without Fathers
What Every Mother Needs to Know
(with Dr. Mardi Allen)

Faith Hill
The Long Road Back

That's Alright, Elvis
The Untold Story of Elvis's First Guitarist
 and Manager, Scotty Moore

Ashley Judd
Crying on the Inside

Devil's Sanctuary
An Eyewitness History of Mississippi Hate Crimes
(with Alex A. Alston Jr.)

Mojo Triangle
Birthplace of Country, Blues, Jazz and Rock 'n' Roll

Trader Jon's
Cradle of U.S. Naval Aviation

Last Dance at the Sudden Death Café (novel)

Legend of the Soul Eater (novel)

Love on the Rocks: Romance to the Rescue (novel)

Two Women, One Man: A Memphis Love Story (novel)

Natalie Portman's

Stark Reality

A BIOGRAPHY

JAMES L. DICKERSON

SARTORIS LITERARY GROUP

SARTORIS LITERARY GROUP
www.sartorisliterary.com

Contents

Photofest

Chapter 1

Making Sense of Chaos

"My beautiful granddaughter is a conehead!"

Natalie was born five days late—and, oddly enough, *on her mother's 29ᵗʰ birthday*. When Natalie's doting Israeli grandmother walked into the hospital room, she was surprised by baby Natalie's appearance. Her head was elongated, shaped like a cone. The delivery had been unexpectedly difficult, and doctors had been forced to use an obstetrical vacuum to help Natalie make her way through the birth canal. The process had distorted her head somewhat, making her stand out from the other babies in the nursery.

Grandmother Hershlag could not help herself. She had to comment.

Years later, while relating the story to actress Susan Sarandon, who interviewed Natalie for *Jane* magazine, Natalie said she had good-naturedly complained to her father about her grandmother calling her a conehead. He had laughed and said, "You should've heard what she said about *me*," explaining that she had labeled him the "ugliest" baby she had ever seen.

Of course, references to Natalie being a "conehead" are laughable today. Her mother is a striking woman, as you might expect, and her father, balding but clean-shaven, is a handsome man with a compassionate face and a smile almost identical to Natalie's.

Long before there was ever a Natalie Portman there was Natalie Hershlag. Born June 9, 1981, in Jerusalem to her Israeli-born father, Dr. Avner Hershlag, and her American-born mother, Shelley, Natalie Hershlag was brought into a world of competing, sometimes opposing, religious, political and cultural ideologies.

Was she Israeli? American? Jew? Or something else entirely?

Certainly, she was a Jew—and proudly so. But she had United States *and* Israeli citizenship. Much of her life has been spent trying to define herself, both internally and externally. As it turns out she is all of the above possibilities—and more.

Look into the face of either parent and you will see bits and pieces of Natalie. From a personality standpoint, Natalie is a composite of her parents. Natalie's mother, Shelley, is a sensitive woman with an artistic temperament, and her father, Avner, is a scientific-minded physician and aspiring novelist. They prove the old adage that opposites attract. That adage can be extended to Natalie herself, who is a composite of opposing personality traits.

On her father's side, Natalie has a Jewish pedigree second to none. With roots in Rzeszow, Poland, the Hershlag family has a history of fierce Zionism. Avner's parents moved to Israel in the late 1930s from Poland, where they were ethnically proud, politically active Jews in Poland who, like the American Minutemen during the Revolutionary War, stood both *for* an independent homeland and *against* the oppression of their religious beliefs. His grandfather headed the Jewish youth movement in Poland and his Romanian grandmother, an attractive woman who passed for a non-Jew, spied for the British as she traveled throughout Europe.

In some respects the Hershlags were the Paul Reveres of early Zionism. Sadly, when Avner's father came to Israel, it was his intention to send for other family members. However, the German Nazi Party intervened and his other family members were sent to the concentration camp in Auschwitz.

Since 1921, when Adolf Hitler became the leader of Germany's National Socialist Party (Nazi Party, for short), Jews had been blamed for a wide range of social and economic ills. The Hershlags had seen it all before. For centuries, they had settled in Europe. Jews, driven out of Palestine two thousand years ago by the Romans, had gravitated toward Europe, where for fourteen centuries they had been persecuted by Christians and blamed for an assortment of societal ills and catastrophes, including the Black Death, a disease that destroyed nearly a quarter of the entire population of Europe. By the fourteenth century, the only place they were welcome was Poland, where a benevolent kingdom offered them a level of cultural tranquillity not afforded Jews in other nations. They were allowed to practice their religious beliefs and to live apart from the Christian population. They undertook a wide range of occupations, but mostly they focused on money lending and tax collection, professions at that time considered beneath the dignity of Christians.

By the mid-1600s, half the Jews in the world lived in the joint kingdom of Poland and Lithuania. Almost three hundred years of peace and prosperity came to an end in 1648 when a Ukrainian uprising against the Polish nobility and the Roman Catholic Church resulted in the deaths of nearly one-third of the Jewish people in Poland. Jews were targeted because they were the "killers of Christ" and because they collected taxes from the Ukrainians on behalf of Polish landlords.

"These persons [Jews] died cruel and bitter deaths," wrote one contemporary chronicler in *The Abyss of Despair*. "Some were skinned alive and their flesh was thrown to the dogs. . . . The enemy slaughtered infants in the laps of their mothers. They were sliced into pieces like fish. They slashed the bellies of pregnant women, removed their infants and tossed them in their faces. . . . Some children were pierced on spears, roasted on the fire, and then brought to their mothers to be eaten."

The Ukrainian massacre sent many Jews fleeing into Germany, where 250 years later they became targets of the Nazis. However, most Polish Jews, including the Hershlags, remained where they were and lived in social and cultural isolation. It was not an easy life, for they were always on guard for the next round of persecution.

By the early 1930s, when Avner's father moved to Israel, he had been subjected to nearly a decade of Nazi propaganda in nearby Germany. Jews were blamed for the worldwide economic depression. Many German Jews returned to Poland during that time, where they were encouraged to strengthen existing Jewish communities rather than emigrate to other European countries. Many Polish Jews wanted to flee to the United States, but immigration laws were strict, and Jews were not welcome in America during the economic hard times of the late 1920s and 1930s.

Natalie's ancestors, including her great-grandfather, were murdered in Auschwitz, and her father's uncle was murdered in the streets of Rzeszow. They never lived to see their dreams of a Jewish state come true, but some of the children survived the Holocaust, managing to escape to Palestine before the Germans invaded Poland.

At the end of World War II, much of the world's focus was on what to do about the liberated Holocaust victims and the millions of Jews who had fled Nazi Germany. The United States allowed some Jews into the country, but most of the Jews who sought refuge were turned away at the embassy level. Those who came anyway were interned in prison camps in New York, some for up to two years. It was not America's finest hour.

Zionists saw a way to turn tragedy into triumph. Recognizing that few nations wanted the millions of refugees displaced by the war, Jewish leaders pressured Great Britain, which had ruled Palestine since 1922 under a mandate from the United Nations, to allow the Jews into Palestine. It was a tough sell since the British had prohibited Jews from entering Palestine during the war.

Zionists counted on pressure from the United States, already turning away Jews by the thousands, to find a solution. America's argument to Great Britain was pragmatic: if neither country was prepared to take the Jews, then they had no choice but to find them a country of their own. Great Britain turned the problem over to the United Nations for resolution. The solution, as determined by the United Nations, was that Palestine should be divided into two independent states, a Jewish state and an Arab state. In May 1948, the British withdrew from Palestine, allowing the Zionists to proclaim the new state of Israel.

*   *   *

By the time Natalie was born in 1981, Israel had undergone many changes in the thirty-three years since its creation. In the 1967 "Six Day War," Israel's potent military machine captured enough Palestinian and other Arab land to quadruple its territorial boundaries. Included in that conquest was the capture of Jerusalem, which the United Nations in 1948 had designated open to all nationalities in the region.

Natalie's birth in Jerusalem had deep meaning for the Hershlag family. The Hebrew word for Jerusalem is Zion, a city that has been the focal point of Zionism for the past 1,900 years. The Hershlags had big plans for Natalie. She was a symbol of all that they had become and hoped to be.

In keeping with family tradition, Avner Hershlag had served in youth organizations, including the International Federation of Medical Students Society, in which he had eventually been elected director of medical education. When Natalie was born, Avner had just completed his training at the Hadassah Medical School in Jerusalem. For the next three years, he held a general surgery residency at the Hadassah hospital. At the end of that residency, he had a major decision to make: he wanted to continue his education by specializing in obstetrics and gynecology. His family wanted him to do it in Israel, but Shelley wanted him to do it in the United States, where she hoped they would make a home for their new family.

Since her father was Israeli and her mother was American, Natalie was born with dual citizenship. However, to retain her American citizenship, she had to reside in the United States for a prescribed number of years prior to her eighteenth birthday. As much as Shelley loved Israel, she could not see her daughter being raised in a communal kibbutz and then drafted into the Israeli army, as all Israeli men and women are required to do at the age of eighteen. Shelley had been raised in Cincinnati in the dark shadow of the Vietnam War, when militarism and the draft had been universally opposed by American youth. The thought of giving her precious daughter up to a kibbutz and then the Israeli military went against everything she believed in as an American.

By Natalie's third birthday, when Avner completed his residency at Hadassah, it was apparent that major decisions would have to be made. He wanted to continue his education, but that would mean a commitment of up to four years. If he made that commitment in Israel, then Natalie would become of age for entry into a kibbutz. While there was no law dictating that she submit to the kibbutz system, the fact that the Hershlags had been among the founders of the first kibbutzim put pressure on Avner to consider that possibility for his daughter.

Shelley suggested that they move to America, where Avner could pursue his education and Natalie could be raised as she herself had been brought up. Natalie's maternal grandparents wholeheartedly backed that proposal. Against it, of course, was Avner's mother, who wanted them to stay in Israel. Torn between the family that had given him life and his new family, made up of his wife and child, Avner made the only decision he could under the circumstances: he chose the future over the past.

In 1984, the Hershlag family moved to America, where Natalie and her mother already held citizenship. In time, Avner would also obtain American citizenship. His mother was devastated, but she understood the decision and respected Avner for it. Years later, she was interviewed on Israeli television about Natalie's movie career. She acknowledged the tug-of-war between the two families over the issue of relocation in America, but she said it had never affected her love for Natalie.

* * *

Avner and Shelley settled in Maryland, where Avner worked on his obstetrics and gynecology residency at George Washington University Medical Center in Washington, DC. His goal was to become an infertility specialist.

When Natalie was five, she was enrolled in a Maryland nursery school. By then, she was fluent in both English and Hebrew. Her first words had been Hebrew, but her mother, mindful of the importance of being bilingual, had taught her English.

Natalie was a cute little girl, but it was not her looks that set her apart from the other children. It was her *mouth* that got her the most attention from teachers. The students were asked one day what their fathers did for a living. Natalie gleefully told the classroom that her father helped women to get pregnant. She couldn't explain it beyond that. Horrified school officials called Shelley to investigate her home situation. Embarrassed by the implications of the school's query, Shelley explained that Natalie's father was studying to become an infertility specialist. School officials took a deep breath and chased after other windmills.

From Maryland, Natalie's family moved in 1988 to New Haven, Connecticut, where Avner received a fellowship at Yale University to continue his studies in reproductive endocrinology. He quickly made a name for himself as a rising star in the field of infertility medicine, perhaps motivated by the fact that Shelley wouldn't be able to give him additional children of their own.

From an early age, Natalie was a "daddy's girl." Avner made time for her both at home and at work. She went everywhere with him. When she was eight, she accompanied him to a medical conference at which laser surgery on a chicken was demonstrated. She was so horrified when the chicken was killed during the demonstration that she vowed never to eat meat again.

Perhaps as a compromise to her Israeli heritage, Natalie was enrolled in a Jewish school so that she could be educated in the Hebrew tradition. By all accounts, she was a precocious child who exhibited considerable verbal dexterity from an early age.

Once, while Natalie was hanging out at her father's office, Avner allowed her to sit in on an interview with a patient. A question arose about the woman's due date, so he checked on his computer to see when the woman had been inseminated. It had been September 17, ironically the same date he had been born. Then he calculated the woman's due date— June 9, the same date Natalie and her mother had been born.

Avner and Natalie later discussed the mind-boggling oddity of the experience. What she learned from that encounter with the patient (she has always thought it was chance, but a cynic could be forgiven for thinking it might have been a calculated "lesson" in human reproduction) was that, while her father was being born, her mother was being conceived—and, perhaps more important, that she herself had been conceived on her father's birthday. Her response to her father, as she later recalled to *Jane* magazine, was an early indication of her devilish wit: "Dad, I know what *you* got for your birthday."

*   *   *

Shelley enrolled Natalie in dance classes at the age of three while they were still living in Maryland, and she encouraged her to sing and to act out her feelings. Art was not simply something to gaze at or listen to, Shelley taught her daughter: it was a natural form of expression and could be communicated physically in dance. When the family moved to New Haven, Natalie continued her dance lessons and enrolled in a Jewish school, where she could be taught the fundamentals of Judaism in addition to academics.

Natalie's maternal grandfather, Art Stevens, died when Natalie was seven, and she thought nothing of entertaining other family members at his funeral by performing skits she had worked up in her dance class. If it is possible for individuals to have show business in their "blood," as some people believe, then Natalie was an example, though where that bloodline came from was a mystery to everyone in her family.

Natalie's first media exposure occurred when a New Haven dance supply company stopped by her dance class to find models for its catalog. Natalie was among those chosen, and she threw herself into the photo sessions with enthusiasm. Of course, being chosen for the catalog was not exactly a huge compliment since dance supply businesses are usually family owned and models are typically selected from family members or neighborhood children.

But in this instance, Natalie's catalog appearance had a beneficial effect because her photos came to the attention of Wilhelmina Models, a top New York modeling agency that had launched the careers of Whitney Houston, Lauren Hutton, Jessica Lange, Daisy Fuentes, and Sarah Michelle Geller. Natalie was signed by the agency in the late 1980s to its kids division, according to Kristie McCormick, a spokesperson for Wilhelmina Models. Most of the bookings for child models are not lucrative, explained McCormick, perhaps in the seventy-five-dollar range, but they do open doors to bigger things, and that is why large agencies such as Wilhelmina Models invest time in them.

Natalie was far from being a star, but she was now on her way.

*　　*　　*

In 1990, Natalie's family moved to Long Island, New York, where they settled near the small community of Syosset (population 18,967). In New Haven, they had lived not far from the northern shores of Long Island Sound, and on Long Island they found a comfortable, two-story house in an upper-middle-class neighborhood not far from the southern shores of the sound. The house, complete with a basketball hoop, is surrounded by trees and has a suburban air about it, accented by a mixed-breed dog named Noodles that can occasionally be spotted sniffing about the lawn.

Avner accepted a position as medical director of the In Vitro Fertilization Program at the North Shore–Long Island Jewish Center for Human Reproduction at North Shore University Hospital, a facility located in the community of Manhasset, about a forty-five-minute drive from his home. Opened in 1976, the hospital is a world-renowned facility with a reputation for cutting-edge technology and surgical techniques.

Avner also joined the staff of New York University School of Medicine, where he accepted a position of associate professor of obstetrics and gynecology. Within a short time of his arrival in New York, he established himself as a rising star in the field of infertility. Over the next few years, he wrote articles for medical journals and contributed chapters to medical texts on a wide range of subjects within that field.

One of the medical issues that concerns Avner is the multiple births that occur as a result of infertility treatments. No one who goes to a doctor for infertility treatments does so with a desire to have triplets or quadruplets, yet they are a frequent side effect of the treatments. It can be a problem if the couple has limited health-care coverage or financial resources to provide for the sudden arrival of three, four, or five babies.

Some doctors argue that the problem is so serious—multifetal pregnancies are at high risk for birth defects, growth retardation, and death—that a plan should be discussed with patients before treatment is even administered about what to do in the event of multiple fetuses. Those doctors argue that, if such patients do not agree in advance to abort some of the fetuses, then treatment should be denied. Avner disagrees with that position on the grounds that it is tantamount to coercion. Instead, he suggests that doctors lobby insurance companies and lawmakers to expand insurance coverage of infertility treatments so that patients are not so desperate to fertilize as many eggs as possible during treatment.

By the time Natalie became a star, Avner was a star in his own right; he was to medicine what Natalie was to motion pictures. Natalie was well aware of his growing status as a doctor, and even as a child she reveled in his success.

As Avner had done in New Haven, he allowed Natalie to visit him at his office in Manhasset. Since the Long Island Railroad went directly to Penn Stations, only a thirty- minute ride, his office provided a good launching pad for Natalie's modeling excursions into Manhattan.

Whether or not Natalie's parents ever consciously developed a specific, step-by-step plan for raising their daughter, they certainly acted one out. Avner believed it was his responsibility to develop her intellectual skills, especially as they related to math and science. And, since he wanted her to know about life as it is and not as it should be, he talked to her as if she were an adult, and he introduced her to experiences that were beyond the reach of her peers. For example, to teach her about her own body, and the pain and joy of motherhood, he allowed her to observe him in the delivery room on several occasions. Thanks to her father, Natalie saw things that some people live a lifetime without ever experiencing. Natalie's education by her mother was just as deliberate, but it focused on an entirely different side of her development. It was as if her parents divided her brain into two parts, with each parent taking one half to nourish. Shelley thought it was important for Natalie to develop her artistic talents and, along with them, her skills of self-expression, both emotional and physical.

When the family moved to Long Island, Natalie was enrolled in a Jewish school, but her days of being educated in the Hebrew tradition were numbered. She soon became frustrated with the small classes and the limited social interaction offered by a Hebrew education. However, she never lost interest in speaking Hebrew and used it to communicate with her father, while addressing her mother in English.

To an outside observer, that might seem to be a stressful situation for a child, but there is no indication that was ever the case in the Hershlag household. While Natalie's parents addressed different, sometimes opposing, aspects of her development, they did not put their daughter in a position where she had to choose between satisfying the wishes of one parent at the expense of the other.

Natalie's greatest bond with her mother was over their mutual love of drama, whether expressed physically as dance or verbally as dialogue in a play. As her father encouraged Natalie to look inward, to develop her brain and her concept of self, her mother encouraged her to reach out, to develop her heart and her concept of humanity. It sounds daunting, but the practical result of pushing her to polar opposites was to keep her grounded in the center.

When the Hershlags moved to Long Island, Natalie continued the dance lessons she had begun in Maryland and sustained during the two years they lived in New Haven. Dancing was her passion. She dreamed of becoming a professional dancer, not a high-kicking Rockette, but one who could bring audiences to tears or laughter with the calculated movements of her body. Bob Fosse was her favorite director, and when she dreamed of stardom as a dancer it was in Fosse musicals such as *Cabaret, Damn Yankees*, and *Sweet Charity*.

Aware of her dream of becoming a Broadway dancer, but equally aware of the fact that at nine and ten Natalie showed little promise of being much over five feet in height as an adult, her mother encouraged her to pursue acting and, to a lesser degree, modeling (her small stature was a mark against her there as well). Perhaps with that in mind, Shelley enrolled Natalie in the Usdan Center for the Creative and Performing Arts in Huntington, Long Island. It was a day camp that each summer took about 1,400 children from metropolitan New York and taught them the basics of art, dance, music, and theater.

Usdan was never meant to be a pre-professional training school in the arts, and its students were chosen from families with diverse social and economic backgrounds. Natalie was only one of 1,400 students, but she excelled in her drama classes and landed roles in camp presentations, playing Annie in *Annie Get Your Gun* and a dumb blonde named Dora in *Fiorello*. Since Usdan ran only for the summer months, Natalie continued her private dance lessons. Maybe she would never become a tall, leggy dancer, but the important thing was that it gave her pleasure to dance. Even at an early age, she learned there are some things you do just for yourself.

One day in 1991, when Natalie was ten, her mother picked her up after her dance class, and they went to a local pizza parlor to get a bite to eat. They soon became aware of a man staring at them from across the room. Neither Natalie nor her mother is gregarious when it comes to interacting with strangers in public, so they nearly bolted for the door when the man rose from his seat and approached their table. He introduced himself and said he was a representative from Revlon.

Yeah, sure, Natalie thought.

The man complimented Natalie on how pretty she looked and explained that Revlon was searching for young models for an upcoming advertising campaign. He thought she would be perfect. He gave Shelley his business card and encouraged her to give him a call if they were interested in pursuing the opportunity.

"You've got a beautiful face," he told Natalie. "You could be a star!"

Photofest

Chapter 2

Natalie Goes Professional

Natalie may have had the face of an angel, but inside she was a lit firecracker. She thought her photographs should be entertaining, you know, display a little personality, but that was not what the photographers wanted.

"Stand still and smile," she was told.

"Now look serious . . . now look pretty."

Natalie was bored senseless by the experience. She hated every minute of it. She didn't want to be a mannequin. People did not laugh or cry when they looked at mannequins. They simply stared, as if they were slabs of meat.

Despite the interest shown in her by Revlon, Natalie told her agent at Wilhelmina Models that she wanted to be an actor, not a model. So she severed her relationship with the modeling agency in order to focus on acting. She signed with a new agent who worked with actors.

Of course, there is an enormous difference between modeling and acting, in both content and lifestyle. After child models participate in one-day photo sessions and the results are published or broadcast, almost always without their names attached, they go about their normal routines with a high degree of anonymity. But the same is not true for child actors. When they take on an assignment, it can be for weeks or months at a time, and anonymity goes out the window. Their work is reviewed, and their names are associated with the product.

The first decision the Hershlag family had to make was about Natalie's last name. Should she use her birth name or devise a stage name? *Natalie*

Hershlag didn't have the ring of Elizabeth Taylor or Jane Fonda or Marilyn Monroe. Was it too ethnic for the American public to accept? Natalie worked as a first name, as evidenced by the success of Natalie Wood in the 1950s and 1960s, but Hershlag was a name that does not automatically roll off the lips.

There were other considerations for the family. Avner had a splendid career ahead of him as a doctor. Did he really want that proud Jewish name to be associated with the movie business? Then there was Natalie's young age. If Natalie used her birth name, would stalkers and others try to take advantage of her?

In the end, it was the final consideration that had the most influence. Natalie was an only child. Her overprotective parents, who had genuine fears, urged her to use a stage name, one that would deflect attention away from their private lives and careers. Having a secret identity appealed to the actor in Natalie, so she tried on names the way one might appraise hats. The name with the most resonance was the one she borrowed from her maternal grandmother, Bernice Stevens, whose maiden name was Portman. It had just the right mix of consonants and vowels.

Natalie Hershlag of Jerusalem was born again on Long Island and unleashed on an unsuspecting world as *Natalie Portman*.

*   *   *

In 1956, when children said "yes, ma'am" and "no, sir" and uttered profanities only beneath the covers of their Mickey Mouse bedspreads, one of the biggest movies going around was *The Bad Seed*, a thriller about a demonic preteen girl who was the personification of evil (at least by 1956 standards). In 1992, *The Bad Seed* resurfaced as an off-Broadway musical named *Ruthless*.

Starring eleven-year-old newcomer Laura Bundy as Tina Denmark, the scheming child from hell, *Ruthless* opened at the Player's Theatre in New York's Greenwich Village to enthusiastic reviews. Said drama critic Robert Feldberg of the New Jersey *Record*, "It is aggressively outrageous, right down to the tapping toes of little Tina Denmark . . . who will do anything to win the big part in her school show, 'Pippi in Tahiti: The Musical,' including murdering the leading lady."

Homicide has its drawbacks, of course, and when her crime is discovered Tina is sent packing to a reform school, where she serves four years in detention. Upon her return, she seems to be a chastened young woman. But underneath the smiles and polite language beats the heart of a ruthless psychopath who is still committed to doing whatever it takes to get her way. It may be helpful at this point to remember that *Ruthless* is a musical comedy with songs written by Melvin Laird and director Joel Paley. Despite the stench of homicide and the devilish scheming, there is a lot of singing and the occasional kicking up of heels.

Critic Feldberg was smitten by Laura's performance, proclaiming that her squeaky voice and "ice-cold stare" gave him goose bumps and a laugh at the same time. Laura was "unlike any child you've seen on-stage or off." Most New Yorkers felt the same way. Child actors who impact the dramatic landscape do not come along often, but when they do they usually attract a lot of attention.

Laura Bundy had arrived at *Ruthless* in a manner that was entirely familiar to Natalie and her parents. Starting with a contract with the Eileen Ford Modeling Agency at the age of five, the green-eyed blonde had attended the Professional Children's School and, for six years, made the audition rounds until she had landed the role of Tina Denmark.

In the spring of 1992, Natalie was subjected to a steady stream of publicity about Laura, almost all of it adoring. When *Newsday* staff reporter Jeff Bertinetti interviewed the "pretty" girl for its Long Island edition, he began the story by predicting that the role of Tina Denmark would make the child actor a star.

Laura's favorite subjects in school were math and science, as they were for Natalie, but unlike Natalie Laura had a hobby: She played with dolls and made doll houses for them. Natalie must have cringed when she read that. She may have had dolls of her own, but never would she have admitted it outside her home.

Joining the production midway through its first year was another child actor named Britney Spears, who signed on as Laura's understudy. Born in Mississippi but raised in Kentwood, Louisiana, a small town not far from New Orleans, Britney had shown an interest in music and dance almost from the time she could walk. Sometimes she sang while she danced. Other times she sang while standing on her head or in the bathtub.

Convinced that Britney's talents were too big for Kentwood, her mother, Lynne, took Britney to Atlanta to try out for *The Mickey Mouse Club*. Since she was only eight at the time, producers said she was too young, but they put Lynne in touch with an agent in New York and suggested that if she was really serious about a show business career for Britney, then she should start at the top.

Six months later, after Britney had turned nine, Lynne and Britney's father, Bryan, took their daughter to New York, via a twenty-six-hour Amtrak ride, where they enrolled her in three years of study at the Off-Broadway Dance Center and at the Professional Performing Arts School. Their friends in Kentwood told them they were crazy, but they knew that if they did not take her then, they never would.

"I really didn't like it at first," Britney told *US* magazine. "And my mom's like, 'Baby, whenever you want to go home, we'll go.'"

Britney and her mother, who was pregnant at the time, didn't have the money to pay for cabs, so they walked everywhere they went, spending hours each day simply getting from one place to the next. Eventually, all that hard work paid off. At the age of ten, Britney was hired for her first professional role as the understudy for Laura in *Ruthless*.

Laura and Britney were alike in many ways. Both were precocious, high-energy girls with fetching faces and an emerging sexuality that was projected but never flaunted, a trait shared by many prepubescent girls born in the South (Laura was from Lexington, Kentucky). Whether it is due to the warmer climate or some other, as yet unidentified, sociological disposition, Southern girls aged ten to twelve develop earlier than their Northern counterparts, not just physically but also intuitively. Sometimes that development is expressed as much in physicality as in sexuality. In the South, ten-year-old girls typically make their *presence felt* when they enter a room. Laura and Britney shared that distinction. When they took the stage, men and women alike felt compelled to give them their full attention.

Britney was delighted to have a role in an important New York play, even if she was only the understudy, but it did not take long for the monotony of being a secondary actor to wear down her enthusiasm. "Even though the part was fun, the process of doing the same thing night after night wasn't," she wrote in her autobiography. "It got a little boring for me. As an understudy, I had to be at every performance whether I got to go on or not (and I only got to go on when the star was sick, which was hardly ever). I had to know every line by heart so I'd be ready at a moment's notice."

28

After almost a year of playing the lead role, Laura stepped aside to pursue other interests, catapulting Britney into the spotlight. Laura went on to theater roles in Radio City Music Hall's production of *The Nutcracker*, *The Sound of Music*, and *Gypsy* and then on to the movies, where she starred with Robin Williams in *Jumanji*, but by the end of the decade her career slowed somewhat, sending her to the television soaps, where she took the role of Marah, Reva's daughter on *CBS*'s *Guiding Light*. So much for the durability of childhood stardom.

*   *   *

Britney Spears's ascent into the role of Tina Denmark made room at the bottom for another understudy. That is when eleven-year-old Natalie Portman entered the picture. It was her first professional acting job, and she was eager to please. However, since the production was nearing the end of its run, Natalie was asked to pull double, even triple, duty by learning not only Tina's part but the parts of two minor characters as well.

Natalie and Britney could not have been more different. Both were bright and pretty, and overflowing with energy, but where Natalie was often serious, Britney was irascibly flippant. Britney sometimes turned her back on the audience and made funny faces at the other actors, cracking them up and sending them into giggles that sometimes brought reprimands from the director who did not see Britney's initial pranks.

The girls were different in another aspect as well, one that would affect their careers later in life. While Britney's budding pre-adult persona was evident in the way she carried herself and projected her claim to a physical domain, Natalie's budding pre-adult persona was based on her presentation of a child's body with an adult face, from which came verbal taunts characterized by wit and veiled understatement. In Britney's part of the country, they would have called Natalie a little firecracker.

Natalie dazzled with her vocabulary.

Britney dazzled with her flirtatious beauty.

Britney eventually tired of the production and decided to move on to other things. "It was a lot of fun to play her [Tina] because she couldn't have been more the opposite of me: Tina is spoiled rotten and she would kill (literally) to be a big star," she wrote in her autobiography. "Even though the part was fun, the process of doing the same thing night after night wasn't. It got a little boring for me."

Things came to a head a few days before Christmas when Britney realized she would have to work on Christmas night. That prospect was traumatic to a little girl who still believed in Santa Claus. She told her mother she did not want to work on Christmas. Mother agreed and she gave her notice on Christmas Eve. Natalie didn't mind working on Christmas, so she took on the lead part abandoned by Britney.

Three days before Britney and her mother left New York to return to Kentwood, she landed a part in *The Mickey Mouse Club*, a role she held onto for two years. Britney went on to become a major pop recording artist whose stage persona depended greatly on her budding sexuality.

In retrospect, it is odd to think that the three greatest Lolitas of the 1990s—Laura Bundy, Natalie Portman, and Britney Spears—were all born within a few months of each other in 1981. There must have been something in the air that year.

Laura never had a huge impact on Natalie's career, but Britney certainly did, even though they never had a conversation on the set of *Ruthless,* because she represented everything Natalie was *against* in terms of the development of her own career. Britney stood as her alter ego, one that by turns challenged her, disturbed her, and taunted her. Natalie wanted what

Britney had, but she wanted to get it on her own terms. Years later, the two women became friends. In 2002 they even co-hosted a New Year's party.

Natalie didn't follow Britney's lead in handing in her resignation. Instead, she was delivered a pink slip when the producers decided to shut down the play. Off-Broadway plays do not last forever. *Ruthless* did better than expected financially, it even won an award or two, and it launched the careers of three young girls.

For Natalie, it was time to move on to her next challenge.

*   *   *

The year Natalie was born, twenty-two-year-old French filmmaker Luc Besson was working on his first movie, *L'Avant dernier*. It was a short black-and-white film starring Jean Reno, a veteran French actor; it was released only in French.

It was almost a fluke that Besson became a filmmaker. For the first eighteen years of his life, he traveled the world with his parents, who worked as scuba diving instructors. As an adolescent, he wanted to become a marine biologist and work with dolphins. That dream came to an end at the age of seventeen when a diving accident destroyed any chance that he'd become a professional diver.

When Besson moved back to Paris, his birthplace, he discovered television and movies for the first time (living on the water with his parents had not offered many opportunities for cultural discoveries). Immediately, he sensed that working on films, particularly those in the action genre, would allow him to combine all the experiences he'd had as a child and young adult. Besson took any job he could land working on films, then moved to America, where he lived for three years. Convinced he had learned enough working in America to produce and direct his own film, he returned to France and began work on *L'Avant dernier*.

31

Jean Reno was the type of action star Besson understood. He was charismatic but not handsome in the Hollywood leading-man tradition. Born in Casablanca, Morocco, to parents who had fled Spain to escape Franco and fascism, he'd made his way to France in the 1960s after the death of his mother. By the time Reno signed on to work with Besson on *L'Avant dernier*, the thirty-three-year-old actor had starred in a number of French-language films, incuding the 1991 hit *La Femme Nikita*, about a tough street girl who becomes a professional killer (later the film was remade into a popular television series starring Peta Wilson).

It was while they were making *La Femme Nikita* that Reno suggested to Besson that he write a screenplay for the professional killer Reno was playing in that film. That sounded like a good idea to Besson. "In the beginning, I wrote it for Jean to act in, but not for me to direct," Besson told Henry Sheehan of the *San Jose Mercury News:*

> **But as I started to write, I fell in love with the story. It began when I decided to balance off his character, this bad guy like a Terminator, with another. I was thinking of everything: a woman, a dog, a cat, a plant and a kid. It came down to saying, "The best will be to take the perfect opposite: Twelve years old, pure, feminine, gentle, innocent." It's like sugar and salt in cooking; put it together and it makes a strange taste.**

When Besson finished the script, he realized he had something different, something deeper, than any of the other action scripts he had written. He went to Reno and told him he had some good news and some bad news. The good news was that he had found a good director for the script—himself. The bad news was that he thought he needed to take the script to America and find a big-name American actor to play the lead.

Reno took the bad news with good grace. He was not well known in America, and he understood why Besson wanted to find an important, A-list American actor if possible. Besson's films hardly ever got good

32

reviews in France. French critics thought his use of violence made his films too American. If Besson made a successful film in America, then ultimately it would help both their careers.

Unfortunately, when Besson took the script to America and presented it to the A-list actors he had in mind, they were reluctant to get involved with the project. The role required not only that they play a simple-minded killer, Leon, who often seems to live in a daze, but also that they depict a romantic relationship with a twelve-year-old girl named Mathilda. To his surprise, they all turned down the role. Besson later rationalized that they were reluctant to take on the role because they thought Leon was too unsympathetic. In truth, they probably rejected the role because of his relationship with Mathilda. In France, where the age of consent is lower than in America, pedophilia is a more narrowly defined area of the law. In America, a middle-aged man who has a sexual relationship with a twelve-year-old girl would be considered a pedophile. No American actor of consequence was ready to take on that dubious distinction.

Even without a major American star in the leading role, Besson was able to put together a deal with Columbia Pictures whereby his production company, Les Films Du Dauphin, would produce the film and Columbia Pictures would distribute it. He returned to France and gave Reno the good news: he would play the lead character Leon after all. In America, the film would be titled *The Professional*, but in France it would be marketed under the title of *Leon*.

Now all Besson had to do was sign up the rest of the talent and put together a production schedule for filming in New York. For the role of Norman, a crooked DEA agent who thinks nothing of murdering fellow criminals who shortchange him, he chose Gary Oldman, a British-born actor with a reputation for physically and emotionally transforming himself

33

into the characters he plays. Known as a master of accents, he'd built his career on playing villains, particularly those of a psychotic bent.

Oldman's private life was almost as interesting as his cinematic life. Married to British stage actress Lesley Manville, Oldman had a manic, wild streak in him that, boosted by his rather large intake of alcohol, led to divorce in 1990. That year he married American actress Uma Thurman, only to fall into the same, self-destructive patterns with his drinking. In 1991, he and actor Keifer Sutherland were arrested in Los Angeles on drunk-driving charges, and both spent the night in jail. By that time, his marriage to Thurman was in trouble, and by 1992 he was again in divorce court. Despite his alcoholism, Oldman always turned in solid performances, so Besson had no reservations about hiring him for the part of Norman. Although he was still drinking heavily while the film was made, it never seemed to influence his work.

With Oldman in place, Besson had to find someone to play a third male lead, the Italian American "handler" who gave Leon his murder assignments. He chose Danny Aiello, a sixty-one-year-old native New Yorker, who had appeared in over fifty films, including *The Godfather (Part II)* and *Broadway Danny Rose*. Besson needed someone who could be both compassionate and threatening at the same time, and Aiello fit that description perfectly.

With the male leads in place, Besson turned his attention to finding the right actress for the female lead. Since the film would be an American release, he needed an American to play the role. Unfortunately, no twelve-year-old actresses immediately came to mind, especially one willing to play opposite a middle-aged man.

Besson decided the best approach would be to hold open auditions in the hope of finding a newcomer who was bold and strong enough to undertake the challenge.

*   *   *

When *Ruthless* shut down, Natalie Portman joined the ranks of New York's unemployed actors, although in her case it was no big deal—there was always grammar school to keep her busy. Over the next few months, her agent tried to line up auditions for her, but nothing stuck.

Natalie was precocious and pretty, but she was not a blonde, and casting directors have shown a propensity for blondes over the years. In the 1970s, it was Jody Foster and Tatum O'Neal; in the 1990s, it was Claire Danes in films and Britney Spears in music.

Finally, Natalie's agent was able to line up an audition for the female lead in a feature film titled *The Professional*. Natalie wasn't given much information for the audition. Sometimes directors provide entire scripts, sometimes only a few pages they want an actor to read, and sometimes nothing at all.

Natalie arrived at the audition a few minutes early, so she ducked into the bathroom to take care of business. When she emerged, she was given a bit of bad news: "You're too young. Go home."

It was all over before it even began.

Later, describing the audition to David Letterman in a hilarious 1994 appearance on his *Late Show*, Natalie realized the part about the bathroom sounded strange, so she tried to laugh her way out of the story. Said Letterman, who wasn't about to let her off the hook, That's the strangest audition I've ever heard of in my entire life."

"I had to go to the bathroom," Natalie said.

"Oh, I see."

"I went home without reading or anything."

"Were you depressed about that? Were you saddened?"

"No big deal," answered Natalie.

"You got to use the bathroom," Letterman quipped. "What do you care?"

To her surprise, a few days later Natalie received a call requesting her to return to the audition. This time she stayed at the audition long enough to do a reading. Again she was sent home without encouragement. Two weeks later, she was asked to return, this time to read on videotape. Again she was sent home. The third time they called, they asked her to read for Besson from the actual script.

Natalie read from a scene in which she returns from the grocery store and sees her parents dead on the floor of their apartment. It is an emotional scene and one of the most difficult in the film. Natalie was required to show guile, fear, and restrained sadness, all before pleading for help from a neighbor her character doesn't know very well. It is one of the most memorable scenes in the movie.

After the audition, as Natalie was leaving, Besson cryptically said, "See ya soon!"

"So I went home and I was like, 'I got it!'" she told Angela-Mildred Sharp of *Venice* magazine. "I was really excited. I was jumping off the walls."

Her instincts were correct. Natalie was offered the part, but before she could sign a contract her parents had to read the script. They were horrified by what they read. As written, the script called for Mathilda to appear nude and be filmed in bed with Leon, the middle-aged hitman. There was also a great deal of violence, including scenes in which Mathilda herself committed murder.

Natalie was opposed to the nudity, but she saw nothing wrong with the relationship between Mathilda and Leon. "Her love for him is the love of a daughter for the father who takes care of her—she's never felt that before," the twelve year old explained to *USAToday*. "She doesn't know what love for her father is so she clings to him like a boyfriend."

In one of the original scenes, Mathilda and Leon are in bed in a hotel room when she tells him she is falling in love with him. "It's strange, being in love," she tells him. "It's the first time for me."

Leon questions whether she is old enough to know about love.

She takes his hand and places it on her stomach. "Because I feel it," she explains. "Here . . . in my stomach . . . it's hot." She tells him that she has had a "knot" in her stomach ever since she met him.

Leon yanks his hand away. He says he is happy she no longer has a stomach ache but cannot take credit for its disappearance. Leon nervously leaves the room. When he returns, Mathilda is in the bathroom. He opens the door and sees her standing nude, brushing her hair.

In another scene, Leon teaches Mathilda how to fire a rifle (her agreement with him is that she will take care of him if he teaches her how to become a professional "cleaner" or assassin). From the roof of a building, she uses a telescopic sight to scan Central Park for a victim. She decides on a fat man who sits on a bench reading a newspaper. Her first shot misses, slamming into the bench. The man looks toward the sound but then returns to his newspaper. Mathilda fires a second shot. This time the bench planking explodes on the opposite side. She thinks she has missed again, but then the man tilts over on his side.

"Bull's-eye!" says Leon.

Mathilda is happy about her first kill but disappointed that the man's death was not more spectacular.

Natalie's parents reluctantly agreed to allow Natalie to do the movie—but only if Besson removed the nudity and the scenes in which Mathilda instigates violent acts. Besson agreed, although, as the Hershlags later discovered, he gave some scenes a slightly more sensual twist than was indicated in the working script. Natalie's mother told James Ryan of the *New York Times* that "Seeing the little sexual twists and turns, which are different from what you read in the script, I have to say I squirmed a little bit."

Natalie left school two weeks early in the summer of 1993 to work on the film, but she figured that was all right since working on *The Professional* was an education in itself. Parts of the film were shot in Paris, while other parts were done in New York.

Working in New York had been a longtime dream of Besson's, but the reality of it proved to be educational for the director. "Buildings are so big, so huge, that the light comes into the street at 11 a.m. and leaves at 1 p.m. It's over," he told the *San Jose Mercury News*. "It's a wonderful city, but very difficult to shoot."

Everything Besson had heard about New York being an inhospitable city turned out to be false. Some of the scenes were shot in Spanish Harlem, where the community welcomed him with a warmth that caught him off guard. Everyone, from cops on the beat to people on the street, cooperated with him on the project.

The film opens with Leon meeting with Danny Aiello's character, who wants him to deliver a message to a drug dealer who has intruded on someone else's territory. During the next five or six minutes of screen time, Leon commits six murders. Afterward, on his way home, he picks up two cartons of milk, his main source of nourishment. It is after he enters his apartment building that Natalie's character, Mathilda, makes her first appearance. She is sitting on a hallway ledge in the stairwell, her legs dangling over the edge as she smokes a cigarette. When she sees Leon approaching, she hides the cigarette.

Leon sees a bruise on her face and asks her what happened.

"I fell off my bike," she answers.

Shortly after Leon enters his apartment, Gary Oldman's character, Norman, makes his first appearance. Accompanied by his henchmen, he chastises Mathilda's father for coming up short on a drug shipment. He lets him know in no uncertain terms that if he does not produce the missing drugs by noon the following day there will be trouble.

Once the crooked *DEA* agents leave, Mathilda's father shows how his daughter obtained her earlier bruise by slapping her hard across her face and sending her to her room. The following day, Mathilda's father seems to be unconcerned about the threat. Leon again encounters Mathilda in the hallway. This time her nose is bleeding. He gives her his handkerchief to wipe the blood away.

Asks Mathilda, "Is life always this hard, or just when you're a kid?"

"Always like this," Leon says.

Mathilda tells him she is on the way to the store and will pick up a couple of cartons of milk for him. While she is gone, Norman and Company return and savagely murder her father, stepmother, half-sister, and four-year-old brother. They are still there when she returns from the store. As she enters her apartment, she sees her father lying on the floor, blood pooled around him. Wisely, she keeps walking until she reaches Leon's door. This is the scene Natalie read for Besson on her final reading. It is one of the finest moments of the movie and demonstrates the depth of her talent.

After a moment's hesitation, Leon allows Mathilda into his apartment, aware that she will be killed if he does not. He tries to comfort her over the loss of her family, but she is in no mood for comfort. She is upset more about the loss of her brother than about the murders of her stepmother, father, and half-sister.

"I was more a mother to him than that goddamn pig ever was," she says.

"Don't talk about pigs that way," Leon answers.

It is at this point that Mathilda bonds with Leon. The remainder of the movie is about her attempts to avenge the death of her brother and Leon's realization that for the first time in his life he has someone to take care of. There is a scene in which Mathilda slips into the federal building as a delivery girl in an attempt to kill Norman herself. Leon shoots his way into the building to save her, and from that point on it is clear that his life is about to spiral out of control as Norman makes finding Leon his top priority.

Natalie was never traumatized by the violence in the film because she could see that it was not real. After the violent scenes were over, she saw the blood-splattered actors stand up and joke about the scenes.

"The best part about me is that I can be doing something and totally believe that I'm in the place and after 'cut,' I'm like, OK, I'm Natalie," she told *Venice* magazine. "It's kind of like hypnosis. You're in one place, and then it's over and you're in another and you don't even remember."

Even though Leon was the hitman in the movie, Gary Oldman's character, Norman, was the most frightening. Natalie was mesmerized by the transformation he underwent between takes, as he went from nice-guy actor to psychotic killer, but she never felt intimidated by him. Mostly, she was in awe of him.

Before making the film, Natalie had no idea who Jean Reno was since she had never seen a French movie. To introduce them, director Luc Besson invited Natalie and Reno to his suite at the Essex House, where he cooked spaghetti for them. Later he took them to Central Park so they could get to know each other. It was an odd sighting. Two middle-aged men walking twelve-year-old Natalie through the park as if she were a trophy poodle.

There wasn't much interaction, though, because Reno kept slipping into character and walking away from Besson and Natalie so he could be alone to brood about the life of a hitman. Left alone, Besson and Natalie fed the squirrels with nuts the director had brought from his hotel room. At one point, he put her on the merry-go-round.

By the time filming ended, Natalie and Reno were friends. She later took credit for persuading him to stop smoking. He was resistant at first, but when she told him how disgusting smoking was for the people around him, he folded. What male of any age would want to disgust a face that innocent?

Although her mother was with her at all times during filming, Natalie did feel some discomfort with the scenes that had sexual content. Perhaps, more accurately, she felt discomfort because her mother *was* there watching her do them.

One scene in particular got to Natalie. It occurs after Mathilda confesses her love for Leon, only to see him storm out of the hotel room. Bored and bruised by the rejection, she goes down to the front desk and engages the clerk in conversation. Thinking that she is Leon's daughter, he asks what her father does for a living. She says he is a composer and then, leveling her seductive eyes at the clerk, adds, "Except he's not really my father—he's my *lover*."

41

Mathilda's performance throughout the film is laced with sexual references, but Natalie never thought they got out of hand. She thought it was more of a love story than a sex story. "I understood what was going on so it wasn't as if I was being used," she explained to Kristine McKenna for the *Los Angeles Times*. "This girl is at an age where she's just starting to learn about sexuality, but there's nothing disgusting in the way it's handled."

In another scene, Mathilda and Leon play a game in which she dresses up as a celebrity and asks him to guess whom she is imitating. She does Madonna wearing an oversized black bra, then she dons a white dress and, complete with blue eyeliner, does her version of Marilyn Monroe singing "Happy Birthday" to the president. The only impression that Leon guesses is Gene Kelly, and that is because he is a fan of old Hollywood musicals and ducks into theaters whenever possible to watch them in matinee. Not knowing whom the actress would be, Besson likely did not write Mathilda's impressions into the first draft of the script. More likely, the impressions are the ones Natalie worked up as a young child to entertain her family and friends.

Besson has a penchant for blending humor with both violence and sexuality in his movies. There is a scene in *The Professional* in which Mathilda pleads with Leon to teach her how to become a "cleaner" (his word for hitman). He says no but shoves a pistol toward her as a going-away present. She says that if he doesn't help her, then she will certainly die that night. He tells her he doesn't think she has what it takes to be a professional cleaner. Mathilda grabs the pistol, runs to the balcony, and fires off six rounds in rapid succession.

"How's that?" she says to a stunned but impressed Leon.

* * *

When Natalie returned to school in the fall, she was a different person. How could she not be? She had traveled to Paris, where most of the interior scenes for *The Professional* were shot, especially those in which gunplay was required. She had walked the streets of New York as an actress when she wasn't being shuttled to Hoboken and West New York, New Jersey.

What Natalie quickly learned was that her worldly and exotic experiences had less effect on her than on her schoolmates. She did not feel different because of the movie, but she was certainly viewed differently by those around her. It was not exactly the sort of attention she relished from her peers. Each day when she returned from shooting the *Professional,* she broke down and cried. She discovered that her "friends" had turned on her and had negative things to say about her. It was jealousy in its purest form, but Natalie was too young to understand that All she knew was that the people that she thought were her friends were, in fact, not her friends. It was a very painful time for her.

Part of the problem was that her classes in the Jewish school were small, about twenty students per class, which meant, if she was lucky, there were about ten other girls in her class. In a group that small, it takes only one jealous person to knock the others over like dominos. Another part of the problem was that religious schools, whether they are Jewish, Catholic, Baptist, or whatever, have an institutional need to discourage students from standing apart from their classmates. There is room for only one star in a religious school: God.

Natalie had too much on her shoulders to be able to deal with jealous or insensitive classmates. Not only was she beginning a career as a movie actress, but also she was maintaining a straight-A average in her studies and, on top of that, continuing to live life as her mother and father's little

43

girl. So she and her parents decided that the seventh grade would be her last in the Jewish school. When she began the eighth grade, it would be at a public school in Syosset, where the classes were much larger, allowing her to better blend in with her peers.

Natalie focused on her studies with the knowledge that, when school was out in May 1994, she would be moving on to bigger and better things. In fact, her agent and her parents had plans enough to keep her busy all summer.

Natalie's first project after *The Professional* was a role in a film titled *Developing*. It was written by actress Marya Cohn, who also directed and produced the film. It was a short film, twenty-eight minutes, about a single mother who learns that she has breast cancer. It starred Frances Conroy as the mother, Natalie as her teenage daughter, and veteran actor John De Vries. It was an odd little film that seemed to have difficulty deciding whether it was about a woman with cancer or a daughter trying to cope with a mother with cancer.

Natalie never explained why she undertook the film. Cohn had never written or directed a film, and her only credit was as an actress in *Vermont Is for Lovers*, a 1992 film directed by John O'Brien. Of that film, the *Washington Post* observed, "Actually, some of your better aquariums are livelier and more out of control than it [this film]. Then again, some aquariums are better funded than this no-budget feature debut."

The same could pretty much be said of *Developing*. When the short film was released in 1995, it was not embraced by critics and quickly dropped from the market. Today it appears from time to time on cable networks, usually as a filler between feature films, but it has never been available for sale on videotape.

The experience was not wasted on Natalie, however, because her brief relationship with Cohn planted seeds that grew in later years. Cohn, in her twenties when she made *Developing*, was a graduate of Harvard University, where she was awarded the Louis Sudler Prize in the Arts in 1987. The award is presented each year to the senior student who has demonstrated the most outstanding artistic talent and achievement in film, music, drama, dance, or visual arts. Natalie had not given much thought to what she would do after graduation from high school because that day seemed like a lifetime away, but when work on *Developing* was completed she started thinking more about college, especially Cohn's alma mater.

In the summer of 1994, in addition to her role in *Developing*, Natalie enrolled in Stagedoor Manor Performing Arts Camp. Located in the Catskills resort area, about one hundred miles northwest of New York City, the camp takes "artistically gifted" boys and girls between the ages of eight and eighteen and teaches them the basics of theater and dance. The students live in a converted resort hotel during the term of the camp, which varies for individual students from three to nine weeks.

Instruction at the camp is not rigid, and each student is allowed to choose his or her own schedule. The most talented students are allowed to perform in a stage production of a play chosen by camp directors. For Natalie's class, the play was Lucy Maud Montgomery's *Anne of Green Gables*.

Natalie played the part of Anne, an eleven-year-old orphan who travels to Prince Edward Island, Canada, to live with Marilla and Matthew Cuthbert, an adoptive family she has never met. When she arrives at the train station, no one is there to greet her. That is because the adoptive family is looking for a boy. It is not until after the train leaves that Matthew, actually Marilla's brother, realizes that the skinny girl with braided hair sitting alone is the "boy" he and his sister have been promised. Matthew takes Anne home with him so that Marilla can explain the mistake to her.

The Cuthberts try to find another home for Anne, but she is so outspoken in her opinions—she calls a neighborhood lady "fat, ugly, and a sour old gossip"—that they really cannot find a suitable home for her. Ultimately, her friendly personality and vivid imagination win the Cuthberts over, and they decide to keep her.

Natalie shared a characteristic with Anne: when challenged, they both use wit instead of anger as a retaliatory weapon. Natalie was a natural for this role, a fact that was obviously not lost on the casting director.

Natalie's adult personality had emerged at a very early age, a product of the child-rearing division of labor observed by her parents. As a result, Natalie came of age with an intellect and a personality that were part feminine and part masculine, not that she ever had any physical characteristics that fit the latter mold. She had a "mouth" on her like Anne's, but she learned early on to temper it with wit and devilish understatement.

Unlike most girls, who are taught to smile even when it hurts, Natalie learned to mask her emotions in the masculine tradition. She has a luminous smile, but as a child she seldom used it unless she truly meant it. When stressed or uncertain of her surroundings, she has a tendency to set her jaw and speak with minimum animation in her face. She does so in person and when she is acting in a situation in which she is not comfortable.

If you meet Natalie on the street—and she does not know you—do not expect a smile. If you do know her—and she smiles—you will know that you are "in like Flynn."

46

* * *

When Natalie returned to school in September 1994, it was to a public junior-high school in Long Island. She had never attended a public school, so it opened the door to a whole new world of experiences with students of different races, religions, and life expectations. She embraced those new experiences with enthusiasm and optimism.

Not long after Natalie began classes, *The Professional* was released in France to enthusiastic reviews. Little of that enthusiasm filtered to the United States, which was just as well for her. By the time the film was released in the United States on November 18, Natalie had made a good adjustment to her new school.

Reviews of the film were mixed, but when critics made negative comments they were usually directed toward the implied sexual content and the violence. Wrote Roger Ebert for the *Chicago Sun Times*, "Always in the back of my mind was the troubled thought that there was something wrong about placing a twelve-year-old character in the middle of this action. In a more serious movie . . . the child might not have been out of place. But in what is essentially an exercise—a slick urban thriller—it seems to exploit the youth of the girl without really dealing with it." Richard Schickel of *Time* wrote that "The bonding of Mathilda and Leon may be among the strangest in the long, tiresome history of odd-couple movies. The sweetness that develops between them . . . is crazily dislocating, the more so since Besson's French vision of the New York underworld is so eerily unreal."

Natalie did not much care for reviews of the film that criticized Mathilda's relationship with Leon because they seemed to question her and her parents' judgment in agreeing to do the film. Natalie knew *exactly* what the film was about, and it offended her that critics would talk down to her

47

in their reviews. She saw the relationship between Mathilda and Leon as a love story, not a sordid sex tale, and she wondered why critics could not seem to tell the difference.

Natalie's first national television exposure occurred on November 24, 1994, when Natalie appeared as a guest on *The Late Show with David Letterman*. She was introduced as an "eight grader," and the first question Letterman asked her was if she had gotten out of school early to be on the show. Indeed, she had. Her final class of the day had been in "technology," a term that made Letterman grimace.

"What kind of technology?" he asked.

"We have to make cars out of a piece of wood," she explained. "And I was about to drill a hole in my wood, and I was really scared, and I'm holding it, and they're like, 'Will Natalie Portman please come to the front office for early dismissal?' And I went *yes!*"

As the interview progressed, it was clear that Letterman was taken by her poise and wry sense of humor. When they got around to talking about *The Professional*, Letterman said that if he were her parent there was no way he would have allowed her to do that movie because of the violence. Natalie took exception to that and explained, "No, because after you see them lying on the floor with the fake blood all around, they get up, and they're like 'Hi!'"

Letterman asked her if she had attended the premiere in Paris, and Natalie answered that she had. Then she confessed that she had fallen asleep in the theater because it had been her fifth time to see the movie.

"I'm sitting there sleeping, and the director is next to me, and he says, 'Natalie! Wake up!'" she explained. A few minutes later, the movie ends, and the theater lights come on, causing Natalie to rub her eyes. Thinking she is upset because of the movie, concerned audience members run up to comfort her. Asked if she is crying, she answers, "No, I just woke up!"

Three weeks later, Natalie was a guest on *Late Night with Conan O'Brien*. As the Max Weinberg Seven cranked out their rendition of "Thank Heaven for Little Girls," Natalie emerged from the curtain smiling and waving. O'Brien told her how impressed he was with her entrance.

"Oh, thank you," she said, "I'm pumped."

Before Natalie was introduced, O'Brien and his sidekick, Andy Richter, ran a clip about Larry King, who had been a guest earlier in the week. King and Richter had had a make-believe argument on that show, during which Richter had ripped off what appeared to be King's head and had tossed it into the audience. O'Brien, who knew good shtick when he saw it, perpetuated the argument by saying that he thought Richter had been correct to take that action.

After Natalie sat down, O'Brien jokingly told her that Larry King had made a similar entrance. A few minutes later, Richter made a move toward Natalie as if he might go for her head. She played along, pretending she was wary of him.

When the conversation turned to her trip to Paris for the premiere of *The Professional*, Natalie said she had enjoyed the trip but found the food less than appetizing since she is a vegetarian and the French eat things like "rabbits and frogs."

O'Brien teased her about that, saying she had lost her mind.

"Oh, I'm sorry," Natalie said, laughing. "At least I won't lose my head."

O'Brien bounced the bit back to Richter by saying that his sidekick always had a cigarette in one hand and a rabbit in the other, to which Natalie interrupted with "And Larry King's head between his legs."

The audience went wild, and it wasn't clear if Natalie understood the ribald innuendo of what she had said. Never mind, she looked so innocent saying it that everyone concluded that she *totally* did not understand. However, the smart money went the other way. Natalie may not be a Lolita in real life, but she has proved that she has the role down pat.

Toward the end of her interview, Natalie looked directly into the camera and made a plea to her social studies teacher, a Mr. Stein. "Please can I have an extension! I really need an extension 'cause I had to come here. I had to work over the weekend. I have this big report due, and I'm just dying!"

Chapter 3

Moving Up to the Big League

Aided by her startling performance in *The Professional*, Natalie Portman began the new year with intriguing offers, including opportunities to appear in the thriller *Heat* with Al Pacino and Robert De Niro and in the slice-of-life comedy *Beautiful Girls* with a stellar ensemble cast made up of Matt Dillon, Uma Thurman, Timothy Hutton, and others.

Natalie had become what phrase-hungry tabloid writers like to call an "overnight sensation." All the media recognition was fine with her—after all, she had wanted to be in the spotlight since the age of three—but there were aspects of the attention she received that frustrated the fourteen-year-old actress to no end.

In her naïveté, Natalie did not understand why everyone was commenting on the darker implications of her performance in *The Professional*. She was at an age when she believed that platonic male-female relationships were the rule rather than the exception. If her character does not *feel* anything sexual toward Leon, then why would anyone think there is something sexual? It made no sense to her. Natalie expressed some of that frustration in an interview with Ingrid Sischy of *Interview* magazine. "[The critics are] the ones who have the problems," she said. "Like one critic who wrote a really mean article about how my parents should watch out that I don't turn into Linda Blair. The article said something about how my 'budding breasts were provocatively pointing out from a white T-shirt.' I sat there reading that article wondering, 'What movie did this guy see?'"

Indeed, Natalie's parents were criticized for allowing their daughter to appear in *The Professional*. They weren't too concerned about it because they knew more about Natalie than did any of the critics. Like most fourteen year olds, she was literal in her interpretation of life. There was no sexual content in the movie because she had seen none. If she didn't see it, it didn't exist. Her parents had known she would see it that way and had had no reservations about allowing her to be in the movie. Besides, Shelley had been right there with her on the set, ready to intervene if things ever got out of hand.

Even though Natalie was naïve about how others made judgments of a sexual nature, she was devilishly aware of the power she possessed as a child. Two years after playing the part of Mathilda, Natalie displayed that awareness by reprising the role during a lunch meeting with Karen Parr of *Detour* magazine at a midtown Manhattan café adjacent to the Rockefeller Center Ice Rink. Natalie brought up the memorable scene between Mathilda and the desk clerk, prompting Parr to write, "Her eyes brew, and instantly she becomes the dark and troubled Mathilda amidst the Fifth Avenue tourists lunching beside the ice rink."

"He's not my father—he's my *lover*."

Natalie repeated the wicked line from the movie. Then, playfully taunting her interviewer, she broke out into self-effacing laughter.

"I was like, 'Oh, my God, I cannot believe I said that!'"

*   *   *

After auditioning for *Little Women*—and not getting the part—Natalie was surprised to have been chosen for a small part in Michael Mann's thriller *Heat*. Mann, who served as the film's producer, director, and writer, thought Natalie was a prodigy from the moment he met her. "She has a very short amount of screen time to believably communicate a child who is seriously dysfunctional without any overt hysteria or exaggerated dialogue, and she delivers," Mann told *Entertainment Weekly*. "Only someone with serious talent can do that."

Known for his crime dramas, Mann had ambitious plans for *Heat*. Not only did he want it to be a compelling action drama, with lots of physical action and dazzling special effects, but also he wanted it to be a psychological study that penetrated the dark and tangled minds of a master thief and an equally gifted cop.

Al Pacino was chosen to play the role of the cop. The fifty-five-year-old actor was probably best known for his role as Michael Corleone in the *Godfather* trilogy, but prior to 1995 he had delivered a number of breathtaking performances in films such as *Scent of a Woman* (1992), *Sea of Love* (1989), and *Serpico* (1973). *Heat* would be his twenty-seventh film, and he was well suited to play the role of an urban warrior in search of peace of mind. Born in New York City in 1940, Pacino came of age in the 1950s, when street smarts counted for something in an era when teenage angst was celebrated in movies and in a new type of music called rock 'n' roll. As an adolescent growing up in the Bronx, Pacino learned about organized crime and teenage gang warfare firsthand.

Playing opposite Pacino was Robert De Niro, another New York-born actor who was Pacino's junior by three years. They had last been paired together in *The Godfather II*, but that hardly counted since they appear in separate sections of the film. Artistically, De Niro got the better of Pacino in that pairing because he won an Oscar for his performance, while Pacino did not. Before signing on for *Heat*, De Niro had done forty-eight films, including *Raging Bull* (1980), for which he had been awarded an Oscar, *The Deer Hunter* (1978), and *Taxi Driver* (1976). Like Pacino, De Niro had an urban upbringing, a life experience that prepared him for Mann's allegorical combat on the streets of Los Angeles. Although the two actors have only two face-to-face meetings, they are played off one another masterfully by Mann throughout the film.

The movie begins with De Niro and the members of his gang stockpiling the implements of their trade. De Niro steals an ambulance. Gang member Val Kilmer purchases dynamite. Other gang members rendezvous at various locations in Los Angeles. Their target is an armored car with over one billion dollars in bearer bonds. As the gang methodically goes about its business, Pacino begins his day making love to his wife (Diane Venora). After a shower, he informs her that he cannot take her to breakfast because he has a work-related meeting scheduled.

It is at this point that Natalie Portman, playing Pacino's stepdaughter, Lauren, makes the first of four appearances in the film. Her father is coming to pick her up for an outing, and she is upset because she cannot find her berets. The repartee between daughter and mother is classic Natalie. There is a fine line between overacting and underplaying a scene like that, and Natalie hits it right on the mark.

The armored car heist, with its hi-tech tools of the trade, synchronized explosions, and fast action, is trademark Mann, who began his career writing television shows such as *Starsky and Hutch* and *Miami Vice*. After the armored car heist takes place, the pace of the film picks up dramatically as Pacino is placed in charge of solving the crime. Mann skillfully plays Pacino's marital problems off the relationship issues that plague members of the gang. De Niro's love interest is a woman he meets at a lunch counter. Played by Amy Brenneman, who went on to star in a hit television series *Judging Amy*, she makes De Niro question, for the first time, his long-standing rule against entering relationships he cannot terminate on a moment's notice.

Also having relationship problems is gang member Val Kilmer. His wife, played by a blonde Ashley Judd, is tired of being married to a criminal. She seeks comfort in the arms of another man, who ultimately passes information on to the police that results in the gang's downfall. This was Natalie's first appearance in a movie with Judd, but it would not be her last.

While Pacino plays a high-stakes game of chess with De Niro, he plays games of a different sort with his wife. She complains he is not paying enough attention to his family. Responds Pacino, "I told you when we got together you were going to have to share me with all the bad people and ugly events on the planet."

"This is not sharing," she says. "This is leftovers."

Pacino encounters a stark symbol of his marital woes when he comes home one day and finds Natalie unconscious in the bathtub, where she has slashed her left arm and leg in a desperate attempt at suicide. Pacino rushes her to the hospital, carrying her into the emergency room in his arms.

In the end, the battle between Pacino and De Niro navigates through the violence and the tortured relationships to get to a place where the obsessions of the two men duel for supremacy. There can be only one winner, and both men are aware of that. That they risk everything in life to seek fulfillment of their competing obsessions is the stuff of high drama— and Mann offers it up unadorned.

When *Heat* was released in December 1995, critics were generally lavish in their praise for what one called a "three-hour epic." Wrote Edward Guthmann of the *San Francisco Chronicle*, "It's a strange thing that Mann attempts here—mixing pop psychology with explosive violence—but if you can buy his premise, and resist the impulse to shrug it off as facile, overblown theatrics, you'll find *Heat* to be an entertaining, if overlong, experience."

"Although the two share little screen time together, Pacino and De Niro's scenes are poignant and gripping," wrote Simon Cote for the *Austin Chronicle*. "Some might have expected the two to collide like forces of nature, but in a high noon scene that should go down in cinematic history, the two merely talk life and realize they are essentially the same."

Ashley Judd received praise for her work in the movie, but none of the critics seemed to notice Natalie. That is understandable in an action movie with an all-star cast. Natalie's four scenes are right on the mark, but they barely make a blip on the three-hour movie. The role did not hurt her career, but it did not help it either.

*   *   *

In the summer of 1995, after wrapping up her work in *Heat*, Natalie returned to Stagedoor Manor Performing Arts Camp. Like the characters played by Pacino and De Niro, she had her own minor obsessions. Despite appearing in two feature films and an artsy short film, Natalie thought she still had much to learn about acting. She was not obsessed with acting; she was obsessed with being a *good* actor.

Nonetheless, there was something schizophrenic about her existence. One moment Natalie was a schoolgirl enjoying her freedom at summer camp, and the next moment she was a movie star appearing with some of the biggest names in moviedom. She relied heavily on her parents' judgments when it came to choosing scripts, particularly on issues dealing with sex and violence, but even at a very young age she always knew what *she* wanted in the way of a script.

When Natalie read the script for *Beautiful Girls*, she fell in love with it instantly, especially the scenes involving thirteen-year-old Marty. "It's so rare to find a script where the character is my age," she told Lael Loewenstein of the *Daily Bruin*, "and smart and funny—and doesn't have sex."

For Scott Rosenberg, who wrote and produced the movie, Natalie was perfect for the part. They auditioned many girls, but no one came close to her: To him, she was Marty. Rosenberg was willing to take a chance on Natalie, just as he was with director Ted Demme, who had only two movie credits—*The Ref* and *Who's the Man?*—and a couple of television credits, including a 1993 episode of *Homicide*. Rosenberg hedged those newcomer bets with an all-star cast that included Matt Dillon, Lauren Holly, Timothy Hutton, Rosie O'Donnell, Mira Sorvina, Michael Rapaport, and Uma Thurman.

Since the story takes place in Massachusetts and the script calls for snow, the movie was filmed in the winter, when it was thought snow would be available. Fearful that there would be no snow in Massachusetts early in the winter, the film company decided to do the filming in Minnesota instead, where meteorologists assured them that there would be plenty of snow all winter.

As it turned out, there was no snow in Minnesota and plenty of snow in Massachusetts. The film company adjusted by making its own snow. Crew members cut chunks of ice from a lake and ground them into small pieces to be scattered about the landscape. It looked so real that Natalie, not knowing it was from a polluted lake, suddenly scooped up a handful of snow and ate it, sending crew members into hysterics.

Timothy Hutton was the only star Natalie played against. At thirty-five, he was a veteran, having appeared in over thirty feature and television movies, including *Scenes from Everyday Life* (1995) and *Ordinary People* (1980). The son of actor Jim Hutton, he'd begun his screen career at the

57

age of five. Just as Natalie had been typecast as a flirtatious preteen, so too he'd been typecast as a sensitive but troubled young man. It was a persona that had won him an Oscar for Best Supporting Actor in *Ordinary People*. That shared history was enough to ensure that he and Natalie would click on screen.

The other primary male lead was Matt Dillon, who had made a name for himself as a teen actor playing alienated young men in *Tex* (1982) and *The Outsiders* (1983). Thirty-one at the time *Beautiful Girls* was filmed, he had the lingering footprints of disaffected youth on his face, although the promise of creeping middle age also shaped his features.

When the movie begins, Hutton is sitting at his piano in a New York bar counting the money in his tip jar. Clearly, he is not yet where he wants to be in life. When he leaves the bar, he goes to the bus station to purchase a ticket to Knight's Ridge, Massachusetts, where his high school reunion is scheduled to take place. As Hutton is on his way to his hometown, classmate Dillon, who never had the nerve to follow his dreams, is operating a snowplow. Soon it becomes apparent that none of the classmates has what he or she wants in life. Michael Rapaport's character has a wall filled with photos of supermodels. Why should he settle for an ordinary woman, he reasons, when the world is filled with so many truly beautiful women?

When Hutton arrives in town, Natalie is building a snowman on the lawn of his father's yard. Hutton's reunion with his father is strained: all his dad can think of to say to his son is to ask him to watch golf on television with him.

That night, when Rapaport picks Hutton up to take him to meet some of the other guys, one of the first things he says is "Anne's banging some meat cutter." He's convinced that his girlfriend of seven years is being unfaithful.

Natalie's first scene with Hutton occurs the next morning when she finds him shoveling snow outside his father's house.

"How old are you?" Hutton asks.

"Thirteen—but I'm an old soul."

She then asks him why he has come home.

"My high school reunion."

"Heavy."

After chatting with him for a few minutes, Natalie asks him if he is "cool." Taken aback, he responds that he thinks so.

"You are," she says, then shakes her head. "Maybe not."

She dismisses him with a laugh and walks away. Hutton looks bewildered, as if he has lost something precious or found something he did not know was lost.

To Hutton's disappointment, the pre-reunion meetings with his buddies are all depressing, reminders of the failures of high school. Nothing much has changed in the fourteen years since their graduation from high school.

Hutton's next meeting with Natalie is one of the highlights of the film. She asks Hutton if he has a girlfriend.

"Why do you ask?"

"I dunno. You're a dude in flux. If I'm not mistaken, you've come back here to the house of loneliness and tears to daddy downer . . . to come to some sort of decision about life."

"You fancy yourself a perceptive little thing, don't you?"

"I don't know about 'little thing.' I happen to be the tallest girl in my class. I may just grow to be five-ten. I'll be *hot!*"

From that moment on, Hutton is hooked, not so much on what Natalie is as on the promise she represents. Soon he finds himself watching her from the window. When he sees her talking to a boy her own age, he goes outside when the boy leaves. Like a jealous suitor, he inquires about the other guy. Natalie explains that he is just a guy in her class.

"He seemed a little short."

"He's twelve years old," Natalie retorts.

In another scene, Hutton encounters Natalie at a frozen pond being used by townspeople as a skating rink. Natalie did not know how to ice-skate when she arrived on the set, but by the time she left she was able to move about the ice like an old pro.

Hutton asks her where her "boyfriend" is, and she says she is no longer "into" him. Hutton asks if she has found someone else.

"Yep—you."

"What?"

"You're my new boyfriend."

Hutton asks her what they will do about their newfound relationship.

"Alas, poor Romeo, we don't do diddly," she answers with a grin. "You'd go to the penitentiary, and I'd be the laughing stock of the Brownies."

The movie is not about a thirty-something man romancing an underage girl, of course. It is about coming to terms with the disappointments and surprises of life. Hutton's fascination with Natalie is based on both his glimpse into the mind of a "beautiful girl" on her way to adulthood and his realization that he can never go back to that age to capture the moments he has lost.

Natalie teaches Hutton about himself, and eventually he understands that the girlfriend he left behind in New York is the reality of life as an adult. When he tells Natalie toward the end of the movie that they should "stay in touch," he says it with a sense that what he really needs is to stay in touch with himself.

On one level, the movie preaches that it is folly to long for supermodels when there are so many "beautiful girls" available for relationships. On a more cynical level, it points out that men yearn for supermodels because the "beautiful girls" who surround them leave much to be desired. Women view the film as proof that men are silly not to see the beauty inside all women. Men view it as confirmation that interior beauty is no match for a pretty face and shapely figure.

When the film was released in February 1996, reviews were generally good. "*Beautiful Girls* has its share of pretty young things, but this charming small-town gabfest is principally about beautiful boys being boys," wrote Rita Kempley for the *Washington Post*. She called Natalie a "sensation" and praised Hutton for his best performance in years. About the two actors, she says they "develop a mutual crush, but it never goes anywhere inappropriate. Like the film, their relationship is tender, touching and downright delightful." In a *New York Times* review, Janet Maslin described the film as a "companionable date movie" that is a "*Big Chill* knockoff," but she had praise for individual performances, especially that of Natalie, whom she described as a "budding knockout" who is "scene-stealingly good."

It was director Ted Demme who perhaps best described Natalie's performance. "In ten years she's going to run the entire world," he told *People* magazine, "and I want to be one of her assistants."

*   *   *

In September 1995, Natalie's personal life underwent a radical change. She began attending classes at Syosset High School at 70 South Woods

61

Road, Syosset, New York, a public institution of about two thousand students. Comparisons to the Jewish schools she had attended are inevitable. Typically, she'd had about twenty students in her class in the Jewish schools; at Syosset, she had about five hundred students in her freshman class. That was a good thing to her because it meant she had a larger pool from which to draw her friends. To Natalie, that meant freedom to be herself.

Syosset High School is unusual in several respects. Although it is a public school, it is as racially segregated as any school was in the South before the civil rights movement. In 2000, it had an 85.5 percent white enrollment, a 1 percent Hispanic enrollment, a 13.3 percent "other" enrollment, and a black enrollment of only 0.3 percent. Only 1 percent of the teachers at the school fall into the "minority" category. Another thing that sets Syosset apart is its low pupil-to-teacher ratio of twelve, a number lower than the state average. Finally, half of the teachers at Syosset have masters' or doctoral degrees, resulting in a median yearly salary of almost $70,000, far above the state average of $48,115. Perhaps because of those distinctions, school officials are reluctant to discuss the institution with the media. Telephone calls from reporters go unanswered. Syosset High School is located on an island, but culturally and institutionally it exists as an island apart from public schools in other parts of the state.

In fairness to Natalie, there is no indication that she or her parents set their sights on Syosset High School with the above considerations in mind. On the contrary, Natalie was practically desperate to escape the rarefied air of the Jewish schools she had attended. By enrolling in a public school, she thought she was finally entering the real world. She did her best to blend in. She joined the track team and shucked her image as a movie star to become just another of the "girls." Of course, at the school everyone knew her as Natalie Hershlag, student, not Natalie Portman, movie star. She passed for ordinary with little apparent effort.

"Natalie is a normal child who is striving for normalcy," Avner Hershlag told *Newsday*. "It is a tribute to my daughter that she's been able to keep her feet on the ground."

Syosset students seemed to agree. They went out of their way to become friends with her, but they were not pushy about it and gave her the space she needed to grow up like a normal teenager. Natalie made half a dozen friends her freshman year, both boys and girls. She liked to play sports with the boys, especially football, and with the girls she liked to talk about the emotional issues that affected them as adolescents. None of her friends seemed to care one way or the other that she had appeared in movies. It was easy to separate the groupies from the real friends because the latter never brought up her movies.

Everything was not perfect, however. Some students made an effort to give Natalie a hard time. One girl spread rumors about her, telling everyone that people were being nice to her only because she was a movie star. The effect was to discourage students from talking to Natalie for fear they would be seen as sucking up to her. She tried to discuss it with the girl, who always kept a close-knit group of supporters around her, but it was difficult for Natalie to approach her for a private conversation.

Natalie's best friend that year was Rachel Neumann, whom Natalie has described as "really, really, really smart." They shared a lot of interests, especially music. "She's so amazing and so cool," Natalie told *Sassy* magazine. "We're always saying the exact same thing at the same time. We read each other's minds and feel each other's feelings. We can have really deep intellectual discussion, and then the next second be beating each other up and laughing about stupid things."

One evening Avner took Natalie and Rachel to a frothy Alanis Morissette concert, a fatherly gesture that must have given him second thoughts when he arrived at the venue and saw that he was the oldest male in attendance. Of course, like any other father of a teenage girl, Avner was just making it up as he went along.

Unlike most girls her age, Natalie was fairly close to her parents. That's because they treated her more like a friend than a subservient daughter. It was a relationship that gave her problems later in life, but at fourteen it seemed to be perfect.

"The best part about being friends with your parents is that no matter what you do, they have to keep loving you," she told *Interview*. "And no matter what they do to me, I have to keep loving them, too."

That first year at Syosset High School, Natalie tried hard to stay focused on her studies, but doing so was sometimes difficult. She had an easy ride until February 1996, and then the publicity demands for *Beautiful Girls* kept her on the go, sometimes making it difficult for her to keep up with her studies.

Natalie's first major media interview for the movie took place on February 1, 1996, on *The Late Show with David Letterman*. Actor Alec Baldwin was also a guest that night and remained on the set so that he could sit next to Natalie, in effect making a grumpy, old-guy sandwich out of her, with Dave on one side and him on the other.

Devilish pseudo-Lolita that she was, Natalie good-naturedly took full advantage of the situation. She told Letterman that she and her friends had rented a movie titled *Threesome* and viewed it at her friend's house. "There's this scene where they . . . get together," Natalie explained. "And her mom came in right as that scene came on. So my friend jumped up, and she's like, 'This isn't *Reality Bites!*' And she got out of it."

Letterman asked Natalie about school. She said that she was supposed to have an English test that day (Letterman's show is taped early in the evening and broadcast at 11:30 p.m. eastern time), but the teacher had been a no-show. Natalie said she thought the teacher had probably been sick. The assignment was to read a travel book and then write an essay about it. At the suggestion of her history teacher, she'd read Jack Kerouac's *On the Road*, a novel about the Beat generation. In fact, she'd stayed up all night to finish it.

Letterman asked if that was a good book to read in the ninth grade.

"It's like a druggie book," she said. "In every chapter, they do like heroin and coke, and then they said they smoked some tea."

Letterman questioned whether the book would be a good influence.

"My history teacher recommended it to me, and I was like, 'Why did you recommend a druggie book to me?' He's kind of a weird guy, though."

Although her comments about her teacher were well received by the audience, when Natalie went to school the next morning her history teacher told her he was not happy about being called "weird" on national television. According to her, he remained unhappy with her for the remainder of the year.

About two weeks later, Natalie returned to national television with an appearance on *Good Morning America*. Host Joan Lunden told the audience she had met Natalie before because her daughter and Natalie had attended summer camp together at Stagedoor Manor in upstate New York. The object of the interview was to promote *Beautiful Girls*—and that was done with a film clip—but the interview itself was rambling and unfocused. Lunden mainly wanted to know why Natalie had become an actress and how she decided which roles to accept. Natalie was patient with Lunden, explaining it all for the umpteenth time in her life. "Good luck,"

Lunden said at the end of the interview. "I mean, you were absolutely incredible in this movie."

Nine days later, Natalie ended her February television tour with an appearance on *The Tonight Show with Jay Leno*. It was her first time to be interviewed by Leno, and she arrived with a plan of attack (Letterman and Leno have vastly different styles when it comes to dealing with children and teens; Letterman uses their comments to make fun of himself, while Leno tends to engage in one-upmanship with them). This would end up being the strangest interview of Natalie's career.

Immediately after Natalie walked out on stage and shook hands with the previous guest, Dallas Cowboys quarterback Troy Aikman, she went on the offensive. Before Leno could get the interview going, she complained that her chair was uncomfortable and asked if she could change places with him. They switched chairs, and Leno sat next to Aikman, not looking very happy about the transfer. Natalie twirled in his chair once, and then started asking him questions as if *she* were the host.

Slowly, Leno regained control of the interview.

At one point, Leno asked Natalie if she had a pet. She told him about her dog Noodles, explaining that the dog had undergone several operations.

When Leno tried to make a joke out of it by asking if Noodles had undergone cosmetic surgery, Natalie moved the host squarely into her sights. She had learned on the Letterman show that two topics always get her attention—implied sex and talk about body parts, especially the posterior area of the body. Natalie denied that Noodles had ever had cosmetic surgery, but she said that the dog had once got a "thorn in her butt."

Then there was the time Noodles started eating slugs and ended up with her mouth glued shut, so they had to take her to the vet to get her mouth opened again. Finally, Natalie explained, Noodles had had her anal glands removed because she'd been using the scent to mark her territory. With that, the audience groaned.

"She started marking us because she thought we were her territory, and it is this really bad smell," Natalie said. "So we had to get the anal glands removed."

With her "butt" card out of the way, Natalie prepared to drop her "sex" card. She never brought up the subject herself, but she opened the door for it when she told Leno she had been discovered on the *Jerry Springer Show* as a "kid with weird talents."

Leno fell for it. "You were on the Springer show?" he asked incredulously.

"No!" Natalie exclaimed. "You're so gullible!"

To which Leno responded, "This is how old guys get in trouble with young girls."

*   *   *

The summer of 1996 was one of Natalie's busiest. It all began on June 11 with the fifth annual MTV Awards, at which Natalie appeared as a presenter. She did not win any awards for her acting—Alicia Silverstone was the top female award winner, most notably for her performance in *Clueless*—but she created quite a sensation at the podium, where she was paired with Patricia Arquette, who elicited gasps from the audience with her tight black rubber gown. Natalie was dressed more conservatively, but her bright face and poise equally dazzled the audience. Together they were the hit of the show.

Natalie had two feature films to do that year—*Mars Attacks* and *Everyone Says I Love You*—but before beginning work on either project she enrolled in summer classes at Stagedoor Manor. After her schedule for the past twelve months, you'd think she would have been ready to kick back and sit on her "butt" for the first part of the summer, but that was never an option for her.

For one thing, killing time at home with two adoring parents who compete to spend time with their daughter is impossible. They keep Natalie on the go constantly. Besides, she was anxious about her upcoming role in *Everyone Says I Love You*, and she more or less wanted to practice on a musical at Stagedoor Manor.

By the luck of the draw, Natalie received a starring role in the camp's production of *Cabaret*, a musical set in Berlin during Hitler's rise to power. She played the part of Sally Bowles, a cabaret performer who has an affair with an American writer who takes her in after she is fired from the club at which she has performed. *Cabaret* originally opened in New York in 1966 and ran for over eleven hundred performances. It was one of Natalie's favorite musicals and offered her an opportunity to practice her singing and dancing. As it turned out, some of those skills would figure prominently in her upcoming movie role, but she did not know that at the time and was eager for the experience.

Camp was more than simply learning lines and working on stage. It was a time for Natalie to be with her friends in an environment not monitored by her parents. It wasn't that she wanted to do anything wild. It was just that she wanted to be free to make daily decisions without going to her parents for approval.

Natalie and her friend from Syosset High School, Lauren, had fun at camp, even when they were on stage, though sometimes the fun started out as something else. During one performance of *Cabaret*, Natalie and Lauren, along with some other girls, were dancing on chairs when Lauren kicked a little too high and toppled off the chair onto the floor, taking

68

down another girl dancing next to her. Even though Lauren and the other girl were down, perhaps with a broken arm or leg, Natalie and all the other girls kept dancing. Neither girl was injured and everyone was able to laugh at it later, but at the time it looked like a train wreck of major proportions. The two girls slunk off the stage like water-soaked poodles, totally humiliated by their lack of grace.

A couple of years later, Natalie played a videotape of the accident on the *Oprah Winfrey Show*. The audience roared with laughter at the mishap, and then Oprah surprised Natalie by bringing Lauren out on the stage.

When Lauren came out and the two girls tried to sit together on the couch, something spastic happened, prompting Natalie to move up onto the armrest.

"Two little butts sitting on a seat," Oprah smirked.

*   *   *

Director Tim Burton has a comic book approach to filmmaking. There is a good reason for that. He began his career by attending the California Institute of the Arts on a fellowship supplied by the Walt Disney Company. His first job was with Disney, and his first project for that company was *The Fox and the Hound*, a traditional animation film released in 1981, the year Natalie Portman drew her first breath of life.

It soon became apparent that mainstream Disney films were not his niche, and the company allowed Burton to work on his own projects, the first of which, *Pee-Wee's Big Adventure*, was a box-office hit in 1985. That led to *Beetlejuice* (1988) and then *Batman* (1989), establishing him as a major Hollywood player. The early 1990s brought him a string of hits—*Edward Scissorhands*, *Batman Returns*, and *Ed Wood*.

When Natalie was asked to audition for his next film, *Mars Attacks*, she was delighted because Burton was not only one of the hottest cutting-edge directors in Hollywood he had assembled an all-star cast that wowed both Natalie and her parents: Jack Nicholson, Glenn Close, Annette Bening, Pierce Brosnan, Danny Devito, Martin Short, Sarah Jessica Parker, Michael J. Fox, Rod Steiger, Tom Jones, and Jim Brown.

Natalie was given the role of Taffy Dale, the all-knowing daughter of President Dale (played by Jack Nicholson) and First Lady Marsha Dale (played by Glenn Close). Nicholson also played the role of Art Land, a sleazy, Las Vegas developer and hustler. Nicholson had won two Academy Awards for performances in *One Flew over the Cuckoo's Nest* (1975) and *Terms of Endearment* (1983), but in recent years the fifty-something actor seemed to be out of sync with the movie-going public, specifically those ticket-buyers in their teens and early twenties.

Glenn Close was in a similar situation. She made a huge splash in 1982 with *The World According to Garp*, for which she received an Oscar nomination, and she followed that in 1983 with *The Big Chill*, which also garnered her an Oscar nomination. The box-office hit *Fatal Attraction* boosted her acting stock in 1987, but then a string of busts pushed her to the back of the line with moviegoers, especially those in the youth market.

Mars Attacks was written as a spoof on the science fiction, world-is-ending genre that has been a mainstay of Hollywood since the 1950s. The plotline was right out of a comic book: Martians invade Earth, and, while the politicians and the media talking heads debate whether the invaders should be embraced or nuked, society falls apart, and the Martians do the only logical thing and start zapping everything in sight.

Natalie's first scene occurs early in the movie. Close is talking to a decorator about redoing the Roosevelt Room. Natalie is reclining on a bed (she sits or reclines throughout most of the movie), where she is listening to her mother's conversation with obvious disdain.

"Mother," she says. "This isn't your house."

Basically, Natalie's role is to play the only adult in the movie. Natalie mainly does that through sulky quips and snide one-liners in scenes that rarely last more than a few seconds. Her longest scene occurs at the end of the movie when she stands on the steps of the Capitol, surrounded by rubble, and presents the Congressional Medal of Honor to the movie's two heroes. She thanks both for "saving the world from the Martians" and kisses the first award recipient on the cheek.

"You don't have to kiss me if you don't want to," says the second award recipient, to which Natalie responds, "I have to."

Later she asks him if he has a girlfriend.

When *Mars Attacks* was released in 1996, critics were torn between paying respect to a filmmaker they admired and respected—and telling the truth. Most told the truth.

Said Janet Maslin of the *New York Times*: "*Mars Attacks* is just a parade of scattershot gags, more often weird than funny and most often just flat." *Entertainment Weekly* boldly proclaimed that Burton's "comic-strip collage lacks zing; if anything, it's as flat as [what] it's parodying."

Natalie was horrified when she went to a theater to see *Mars Attacks* but not for the same reasons as the critics. "My face became ten feet tall and a pimple that was so small seemed huge, like a mosaic," she told author Jane Pratt.

*   *   *

For some people, Woody Allen can practically walk on water (except, of course, when he's getting in trouble over his relationships with his adopted children). So when Natalie's agent said she should audition for Allen's new movie, *Everyone Says I Love You*, her parents urged Natalie to do it. It was *Woody Allen*, for heaven's sake!

Natalie had reservations because it was a musical, and she would have to sing. There was also the fact that Allen never hands out entire scripts to his actors—only those pages that contain scenes involving the particular actor. To make matters worse, Allen does not always write dialogue. Sometimes he simply writes "improvise" on the script, a cue for the actor to make up his or her own lines.

Finally, Natalie built up the courage to go to the audition. When she walked into the room, Allen extended his hand and introduced himself. Then he introduced her to three other individuals in the room. She smiled and said that her name was Natalie. Allen had never seen any of her movies, but he was impressed by the way she looked, the way she carried herself. Basically, he had only three questions for her.

"Where do you live?"

"Long Island."

"How old are you?"

"Fifteen."

"Are you free for the fall?"

"Yes . . . my school will let me take some time off."

"Thank you," he said. "We'll be in touch."

For Natalie, that was the worst possible type of interview. No one had asked her to read from a script. No one had asked her to sing or dance. *Isn't this a musical?* No one had asked her how she would feel being in a musical. Control freak that Natalie was at that age, it was disconcerting because she'd answered questions she thought were unimportant, and she hadn't been given an opportunity to ask questions and have her fears and self-doubts allayed.

Of course, Natalie was offered the part and said yes.

When her portions of the script arrived, it was, as she'd feared, her worst nightmare. Her scenes were all group encounters, and Allen wanted her to interact with the other actors. You know, make it up as she went along.

Street scenes were filmed in New York City, while the interior scenes were filmed during a three-week shoot in Paris. Natalie used the trip for educational purposes, swinging by the Netherlands so she could visit the memorial of Holocaust victim Anne Frank. Just as some Americans were "children" of the 1960s, so too Natalie was "a child" of the Holocaust. It had meaning in her everyday life.

Everyone Says I Love You was a typical Woody Allen film in that it was unlike any of his previous efforts. That it was a musical surprised no one cognizant of the stress and humiliation he had undergone in the early 1990s over his highly publicized divorce from Mia Farrow and marriage to his adopted daughter, Soon-Yi. Allen had not had a smash hit since the 1970s, when *Annie Hall* and *Manhattan* had made him a cinematic legend. He desperately needed something new and fresh.

For the leading roles in *Everyone Says I Love You*, Allen cast Alan Alda and Goldie Hawn as a wealthy Upper East Side couple who encounter a series of problems involving their family members, including Natalie Portman and Drew Barrymore (who falls in love with an ex-convict her parents invite to a party as a demonstration of their open-minded liberalism). Edward Norton plays the straitlaced fiancé Barrymore dumps in favor of the ex-convict. Allen himself plays Hawn's former husband, an expatriate in Paris who falls in love with the delightfully neurotic Julia Roberts.

The film packed more star power than any Allen had done to date, but the stars brought different levels of box-office appeal to the project. Alda had done twenty feature films, two of them for Allen—*Manhattan Murder Mystery* (1993) and *Crimes and Misdemeanors* (1989)—but he had not appeared in a hit movie since *The Four Seasons* (1981). Hollywood's archetypal "sensitive" man, he was eager to parlay that character into something new in a musical.

Hawn was in much the same position. She had appeared in only ten feature films since her 1980 success *Private Benjamin*—and none of them was particularly memorable. Her best work had been in the late 1960s and 1970s with *Cactus Flower* and *Shampoo*. But, like Alda, she was ready for the challenge offered by a nontraditional musical in which she could fly through the air and, when necessary, reprise the dizzy-blonde *Laugh-In* role that had originally catapulted her to success.

Everyone Says I Love You begins with Edward Norton and Drew Barrymore tossing coins into a fountain and then walking along the street and singing a love song in the old Gene Kelly tradition, with passersby filling in the choruses. All of the actors sing their own parts, with the exception of Barrymore, whose screechy singing voice had to be dubbed by professionals.

Natalie makes her first appearance within moments of the opening song when she emerges from a store and walks down the street with one of her sisters. She delivers one of her first lines—"Please, no humiliating scenes!"—after a boy she has a crush on walks past where she is seated with her sister and a friend.

Natalie's next big scene is with the family over dinner. Alda and Hawn are debating Barrymore's impending marriage to Norton (they wonder if she is too young to get married) with the other children, all of whom have opinions about the marriage. Unlike the others, who are all seated at the table, Natalie stands off to the side munching on a sandwich. Clearly ill at ease in a scene that called for improvisation, she manages to get out only one line, "He's that young snook," a reference to Norton. Mostly, she snarfs down the sandwich, looking every bit like a cat walking on hot pavement. She is lost, and it shows on her face. A few minutes later, she deals with the second scariest scene she has ever had to do—running along the beach in a bikini. Poor Natalie! She likely thought she had died and gone to cinematic hell.

Her most memorable scene occurs when she learns that the boy she has a crush on is interested in someone else. Harking back to her summer camp performances, Natalie screws up the nerve to sing the first lines of "I'm Thru with Love." She delivers them in a strong voice with her eyes closed, and she definitely leaves you wanting to hear more.

The first line of the song is passed from Natalie to Alda to Norton, each of whom adds his own emphasis, until finally it lands in the hands of a black rapper who promptly rips the sentiment to shreds. After that, there is a big dance scene in which all the men and women are made up to look like Groucho Marx. In true Hollywood musical tradition, everyone comes to terms with life and presumably lives happily, if not neurotically, ever after.

Everyone Says I Love You was not her best effort, but Natalie knew that and accepted the limitations of her part in the film. But when interviewers asked her what it had been like to work with Allen on the film, she was typically honest, though always in a self-effacing manner.

"I really liked him [Allen], but I had no idea what I was doing," she told *Empire* magazine. "I need direction, I need help. I'm not a naturally funny person. I'm not good at simple improvisation."

Critics were divided on the film's merits. Rita Kempley of the *Washington Post* called it a "sluggish, sputtering tune-fest performed almost entirely by the vocally challenged." The *New York Times* called Natalie and Gaby Hoffmann, who played her sister, "pert little Lolitas whom the camera adores" but said there was "no urgency to the drama of Mr. Allen's playing one more lovesick older man."

As if patronizing reviews and a slow box office were not discouraging enough, the film later became embroiled in a 2001 lawsuit in which Allen charged his longtime friend and producer, Jean Doumanian, with failing to provide him with regular and accurate information about the film's earnings. There are some situations you just cannot sing and dance your way out of.

Although unhappy about her performance in the film, Natalie appeared on *The Late Show with David Letterman* to promote it on November 28, 1996. When she sat down in the chair next to his desk, Letterman looked into the monitor and complimented her on how nice she looked on the television screen. Letterman had viewed the movie but seemed to be uncertain what to say about it. Natalie said it had been "unbelievably fun," but other than that all she talked about was her trip to Paris to film some of her scenes.

The most fun the two had during the interview was in talking about Thanksgiving dinner. Natalie explained that she is a vegetarian and does not eat turkey. She said that her mother does not share her vegetarianism but makes an effort to prepare meals that will appeal to everyone in the family.

"She makes vegetarian stuffing," she explained, "because generally, you know, they stuff it up the turkey's butt and let the juices all flow in."

With mention of the word *butt*, Letterman stared into the camera, looking shocked and perplexed. "Up the butt," he repeated to bandleader Paul Shaffer. "Is that right?"

Shaffer questioned whether he could say that word on television.

"I'm going to have to talk to Mom about that," Letterman said. "For God's sakes!"

Natalie broke into laughter, as did the audience. When the laughter quieted down, Letterman changed the subject. Toward the end of the interview, Natalie complained that the studio was cold. She held up a pair of mittens she had on.

"You know, you wouldn't be cold if you ate meat," Letterman said.

Natalie was all smiles when the interview ended. Unlike some older women, who are hesitant to do the show because of his sometimes biting comments, Natalie loved doing it. If she were a guy, she would want to grow up to be just like David Letterman.

Chapter 4

Queen Amidala
Takes On Anne Frank

Cinematically speaking, 1997 began with a big bang.

In January, filmmaker George Lucas released a pumped-up version of his 1977 blockbuster *Star Wars*. With new scenes, enhanced visual effects, and a digitally re-mastered soundtrack, it attracted an entirely new generation of fans, most of whom were not even born when the movie first made its rounds of the theaters. Among the first-time viewers was Natalie Portman, who had never seen a *Star Wars* movie, not even on television. She had a professional reason for seeing the movie. She had signed on to be the female lead in a new *Star Wars* trilogy, the first of which was scheduled to begin filming that summer. She had also signed on to do a Broadway play set to open that winter: *The Diary of Anne Frank*.

Natalie and her parents had learned a valuable lesson during the previous two years: appearing in movies with big-name actors is not necessarily a free ticket to stardom. Natalie had done supporting roles in four films in 1995 and 1996—*Heat, Beautiful Girls, Mars Attacks*, and *Everyone Says I Love You*—yet when the reviews came come out she'd hardly been mentioned, except for *Beautiful Girls*, a film, most critics had agreed, was "stolen" by her charming performance. The film she was best known for, *The Professional*, had not featured a single A-list actor.

Natalie also learned that being signed to a movie is not always a guarantee that everything will go smoothly. After being signed to play Juliet in Baz Luhrmann's adaptation of *Romeo and Juliet*, she was released during production because squeamish Twentieth Century Fox executives thought she looked too young for the part. Actually, they were more explicit: when they viewed a kissing scene between Natalie and Leonardo DiCaprio, they said it looked as if he were molesting her. As a result, the role was taken from Natalie and awarded to Claire Danes.

The *Romeo and Juliet* disappointment notwithstanding, Natalie needed more starring vehicles, she and her parents reasoned, roles that would allow her career to stand or fall based not on the work of others but on her own talents.

Star Wars and *The Diary of Anne Frank* represented a major change in philosophy about her film career. And, though there wasn't much money involved in doing *Anne Frank* (that was a project of the heart), Natalie became an instant millionaire when she signed on the dotted line for the *Star Wars* trilogy. What would a sixteen year old do with a million dollars? We will never know, at least not in her case, because her parents wisely socked the money away for her. They refused to allow her to buy anything for herself with her movie money, preferring to treat her like any other teen on an allowance.

"If they say no to something, and I say I'll buy it with my own money, I get punished," she told *USA Today*. All that parental money management kept Natalie grounded (what choice did she really have?).

Rumors have circulated within the industry since *The Professional* that Avner and Shelley, one of whom is always on the movie set with Natalie when she is working, are tough to deal with from an industry perspective, but that is an exaggeration. Industry pros are used to parents dropping their kids off and then going out somewhere to go shopping or get wasted. The family histories of child actors are not glorious ones, and the Hershlags are too astute to leave anything to chance when their daughter's welfare is at stake. If anything, they should be admired for the manner in which they have nurtured her dreams while protecting her reality. It's really not an easy thing to do.

Natalie laughs when she reads or hears that the film industry is going to corrupt her. "I feel like it's kept me more innocent, in a way," she told Leslie Bennetts of *Vanity Fair*. "I wasn't really home when my friends were trying pot for the first time. I was always around adults who wouldn't smoke or curse or anything like that around me. I don't do things that are dangerous to myself."

Natalie depends heavily on her friends for support. As close as she is to her parents, she understands that, when all is said and done, they cannot help her to make the leaps from childhood to adolescent to adult. It is a journey she knows she must make with the help of her contemporaries. Natalie has a unique view of friendship. She has described it as anything that keeps her occupied and adds value to her life. She has friendships with people, but she also has friendships with books, music, and movies. She knows it is a good "friendship" when she thinks she can't live without it.

The best indicator of where you stand with Natalie can be found in her wallet, where she carries photos of her family, friends, and schoolmates. If you make the wallet, then you can be certain she carries you in her heart. Rumor has it she also packs photos of herself posed with Julia Roberts and Drew Barrymore.

* * *

Few people ever set out to become a movie star, director, or producer. It usually happens as a result of something else. Certainly, that was the case with George Lucas, who, after growing up on a walnut ranch in California, left high school with the intention of becoming a professional race car driver. A bad car accident put that dream out of commission, sending him to Modesto Junior College and then to the University of Southern California, where he enrolled in the film school. He excelled as a student filmmaker, making a short, technology-based film that won first prize in the 1967–68 National Student Film Festival. As a result of his festival win, Lucas was able to obtain a Warner Brothers scholarship to observe director Francis Ford Coppola at work. The two men became friends and formed a production company in 1969 they named American Zoetrope.

A couple of years later, with no new films in production for American Zoetrope, Coppola signed on to do a film named *The Godfather*, and Lucas decided to form his own production company named Lucasfilm Ltd. His first project for his new company was a 1973 film he wrote and directed named *American Graffiti*. Starring newcomers Harrison Ford, Cindy Williams, and Richard Dreyfuss, and veteran television actor Ron Howard from the popular television series *The Andy Griffith Show*, it was hailed as one of the greatest teen films ever made.

Buoyed by the success of *American Graffiti*, Lucas began writing the screenplay for a science fiction film in the tradition of *Flash Gordon* and *Planet of the Apes*. Titled *Star Wars*, it was unlike anything else ever produced in that it relied on dazzling special effects and new methods of photography. The concept was so new and daring that Lucas had a difficult time finding a movie company to take it on. Finally, Twentieth Century Fox gave him a green light—but only if he agreed to direct the film for free in exchange for a percentage of the box-office profits. Lucas readily agreed, creating a film that broke all box-office records and won an astonishing seven Academy Awards.

By 1983 Lucas had made two additional *Star Wars* films and teamed up with Steven Spielberg to begin a new franchise of action films about an adventurous archeologist named Indiana Jones. The first in that series,

Indiana Jones and the Raiders of the Lost Ark, was released in 1981, the year Natalie Portman was born.

The final episode of *Star Wars*, subtitled *Return of the Jedi*, was released in 1983, and Lucas put aside thoughts of additional episodes for more than a decade. Since the original series began with episode 4, he still had three "prequel" episodes to work with.

In 1995, when Natalie was only fourteen, he signed her for the female lead in all three episodes. Why would Lucas risk the entire franchise on a young actress who, at that point, had starred in only one feature film, *The Professional*? Because he saw greatness in her as an actress and an opportunity for her to "grow" into the role.

The first episode would be filmed in 1997, when she would be sixteen; the second episode would be filmed in 1999, when she would be eighteen; and the final episode would be filmed in 2002, when she would be twenty-one. Explaining his decision to the *Los Angeles Times*, Lucas said, "Natalie is very intelligent and has a lot of presence and is a very strong person, and at the same time, she's very young. I needed somebody to play a fourteen-year-old girl [in the first episode] who's basically been elected to rule a planet and make that believable."

Despite Lucas's enthusiasm, Natalie was not quick to sign on for a three-movie deal. Having never seen *Star Wars*, the series meant nothing to her. She quickly learned how important the series was, but that wasn't the only consideration. Despite her success in films, she still wasn't certain she wanted to make a career out of acting. The adoring publicity she had received for her films had not gone to her head. Natalie was still a kid, and she understood that. Of equal concern to her was getting an education and finding a niche in which she could be of use to people. That attitude had come from her father, whom she loved and respected.

After thinking over the offer for a few weeks, Natalie agreed to do the movie, but only if it could be filmed in the summer months so as not to interfere with her education. That was agreeable to Lucas, and Natalie signed a contract that committed her to his film company for the next seven years of her life.

In the summer of 1997, when they began filming *Star Wars: The Phantom Menace*, Natalie did not know what to expect. She had never acted in a movie in which technology plays as important a role as the actors or the plot.

Natalie was chosen to play the dual roles of Queen Amidala and Padme. Actually, the two teens are the same person. When Queen Amidala wishes to go incognito among her subjects, she dresses as Padme and has her handmaiden assume her role as queen. Since the queen always wears a painted face in public, the role reversal is more feasible than it sounds. The actress hired to play the role of the handmaiden never actually plays her when she has lines to say and only appears as Queen Padme. Confused? Don't feel bad. Natalie's mother once confused the two while they were on the set and started chatting with the stand-in, thinking she was Natalie.

Before Natalie recited a word from the script, Lucas insisted that two aspects of the character be perfected first. The first aspect was Queen Amidala's look. Since much of the previous success of the movies was due to visuals, Lucas wanted his queen to leave a visual imprint on the viewer. Makeup contributed to the image by giving her an unusual look, apart from the white pancake that covered her face. Natalie had red gloss on her top lip, white gloss on her bottom lip, and a vertical red stripe down the center of her bottom lip. She liked that look but had problems remembering not to press her lips together, the result of which was always pink lips. To keep her lips fresh, a makeup person stayed nearby throughout the filming.

Anytime Natalie had an off-camera conversation or anything to eat, the makeup person was required to re-gloss her lips.

The second aspect was the heavy costume. Because of the weight, Lucas had someone follow Natalie everywhere to be ready to lift the hems of her skirts. So that Natalie could go to the bathroom without difficulty, the costume designer put snaps on the gowns that allowed her to slip out of them in a flash.

For the queen's "sound," Lucas wanted something different from Natalie's previous screen roles. He asked Natalie to work with a dialect coach to devise an accent that didn't seem to come from any specific geographical location. She did her part by watching classic movies starring Lauren Bacall, Katharine Hepburn, and Audrey Hepburn. What Natalie wanted to learn from them was how to carry herself as queen and how to speak with feminine eloquence.

Starring in *The Phantom Menace* with Natalie were Liam Neeson as Qui-Gon Jinn and Ewan McGregor as Obi-Wan Kenobi. Born in Ireland, the six-foot-four Neeson seemed to be an unlikely candidate for a Jedi knight. Although he scored with audiences in 1981 with a role in *Excalibur*, his career had been unspectacular until he'd signed on to play the role of Oskar Schindler in Steven Speilberg's *Schindler's List* (1993), a film that dealt with Holocaust issues.

Star Wars fans were familiar with Obi-Wan Kenobi, the elderly Jedi knight who introduced Luke Skywalker to the power of the Force. In the first movie, he was played by veteran actor Alec Guiness, but this time he was played by Ewan McGregor, who depicted him as a young warrior in training.

When *The Phantom Menace* begins, the planet Naboo is under siege by the evil Trade Federation over what is proclaimed to be a taxation issue.

Concerned that the federation may be up to no good, the Galactic Republic sends two Jedi emissaries, Neeson and McGregor. When they land on the command ship, they quickly learn that the federation has plans to invade Naboo and depose Queen Amidala.

Natalie's first scene occurs when the queen communicates with federation officials electronically to confront them over the siege. Queen Amidala informs them that two Jedi knights have been sent to end the standoff. Federation officials respond that they have no knowledge of that, and they assure the queen of their intention of continuing the siege. Of course, at that very moment the federation is preparing to launch its invasion. In an effort to warn the queen, Neeson and McGregor stow away on one of the invasion ships and descend to Naboo.

Unfortunately, the Jedi knights reach the queen too late to help her repel the attack. Instead, they help her flee to the desert planet Tayooine, where they meet a young slave named Anakin Skywalker (Jake Lloyd). Because he has special skills associated with the Force, the invisible power of the universe, they enlist his help in saving the queen's planet—and, by extension, the entire Galactic Republic. To accomplish that, they must transport the queen to the Senate of the Galactic Republic so she can make her case for intervention.

Since this film represents the beginning of the *Star Wars* saga, all of the major players have an importance apart from their obvious meaning to this particular story. For example, Anakin Skywalker grows up to be the villainous Darth Vader, known to all *Star Wars* fans as the darkest bad guy in movie history.

Natalie spends most of her time in the movie as Padme, without the character restraints placed on the regal queen, but Lucas wanted that character to be somewhat bland, and Natalie delivered even though it went against her instincts as an actress. In retrospect, that might have been the biggest mistake Lucas made in the film. How much better the character might have been had Natalie been left to her own irreverent and suggestive devices.

Dialogue is never the strong point of a Lucas film, and *The Phantom Menace* is no exception. Natalie has no memorable lines in the film, and at times it seems as if she is acting with one arm figuratively tied behind her back. Of course, that may have been part of Lucas's plan all along. Fans will not know for certain until they see the second and third episodes.

Making the film was more grueling than anything Natalie had ever undertaken. Parts of the film were shot in the Tunisian desert, where the heat, often over one hundred degrees, was overpowering. Natalie sprained her ankle during one sequence and was nearly blinded in another when a small explosive charge was unintentionally detonated in her face during an action scene, sending debris into her eye. Luckily, she wasn't seriously injured, but the incident underscored her status as an almost adult actress.

"I'd always been treated like a kid on sets," she told *Premiere* magazine. "Now I was, like, an adult, and I kind of wasn't ready for it. It's a big mind change."

The interior scenes were shot in London, which made the work more pleasant from a physical standpoint, but the isolation worked on Natalie in unexpected ways. She became very lonely. Neeson and McGregor had their wives and children there and spent time with them when they were not filming. Jake Lloyd was only eight, so that left him out as an after-hours companion for Natalie. She mainly hung out with Ahmed Best, a twenty-three-year-old African American dancer who'd been hired to mime the movements of the most beloved animated character in the film, the spastic Jar Jar Binks (he ended up doing the voice as well). After hours,

Natalie and Ahmed went to dance clubs and danced the night away, along with several of her friends and his girlfriend.

Once Natalie dealt with the isolation and loneliness of working in London, she reveled in the implications of playing Queen Amidala. How cool was it to be fourteen and in charge of a planet? Fantasy-wise it doesn't get better than that for a fourteen year old.

After *The Professional*, people said Natalie had "grown up" on the set of the film. That wasn't really true. She was not nearly as affected by the film as the people who watched it. Natalie did not truly grow up until she slipped into the weighty gowns of Queen Amidala and fantasized about ruling the world.

"I think girls are reluctant to become leaders," she told *Star Wars Insider*. "We don't have a lot of female leaders to look up to. There have been very few in reality and very little on film . . . so I think it's really cool for a girl to be in command, to see this young woman in a very strong and powerful position."

*   *   *

If one of the signs of high intelligence is the ability to process multiple, sometimes competing intellectual concepts at the same time, then Natalie has nothing to fear from the high-IQ police. One of her most fascinating personality characteristics is her ability to juggle more than one acting project with her schoolwork and her family obligations. Granted, it is a talent that may have been learned, partially at least, from her enthusiastic parents, who have always presented Natalie with opposing requests of "Do this!" and "No, do this!" Yet that does not lessen her impressive commitment to everything she undertakes. As a juggler of competing intellectual concepts, she is the Tiger Woods of her league.

While Natalie was preparing for and then executing her role as Queen Amidala in *The Phantom Menace*, she was also researching and preparing for her starring role in the Broadway production of *The Diary of Anne Frank*. For an actress with no assistants—she could hardly send a stand-in to her classes to take her exams or onto the track field to run for her—her workload was extraordinary.

By the age of seventeen, Natalie had made three trips to Europe to work on films. On two of those trips, she'd gone to Amsterdam to visit the house where thirteen-year-old Anne Frank and her family had hidden from the Nazis after the 1940 invasion of the Netherlands. Since the Nazis were scouring the neighborhood in search of Jews, the Frank family—made up of Otto Frank; his wife, Edith Frank-Hollander; and their daughters, Anne and Margot—hid in the back portion of the building where his business was located.

"You walk in, and it's like apartment size, [but] when you are reading the book, you imagine it to be a closet," Natalie told *Boston* magazine. "I mean, if I get into a fight with one of my parents, I just have to get out. I have to like run outside. I can't imagine what it would be like having to sit there and not be able to go anywhere, and also not to see daylight—that's the scariest thing."

With little to do in her hiding place, Anne kept a diary that reflected her thoughts on the Germans, her family members, her fear of being discovered, Dutch society, as well as becoming an adolescent. Later the Franks were joined in their hiding place by a second Jewish family in need of sanctuary from the murderous Nazis.

For two years, the Frank family lived in their hideaway, but then one day they were betrayed and deported to a concentration camp. After they were taken away, Miep Gies, a Christian Dutch woman who'd helped to hide them, discovered Anne's diary. She kept it in a safe place so she could return it to Anne after the war.

Descriptions of Anne in the concentration camp are haunting.

"I can still see her standing by the door, watching a group of naked young gypsy girls being shoved along to the crematory," one survivor told *Time* magazine in 1958. "Anne watched them, weeping, and she also wept when we filed past Hungarian children waiting, twelve hours naked under the rain, for their turn to enter the gas chamber. Anne cried, 'Look at their eyes!' She wept when most of us had no tears left."

Unfortunately, Anne died in the concentration camp only weeks before it was liberated by the British. Miep Gies gave the diary to Otto Frank, the only family member to survive the Holocaust. Touched by his daughter's thoughts, Otto arranged for publication of the book in 1947. Titled *Anne Frank: The Diary of a Young Girl*, it has since been published in more than fifty-five languages.

On her second visit to the Franks' house, Natalie met Miep Gies, who was still alive after all those years. Her eyes filled with tears. To Gies, she apologetically said, "I'm sure everyone cries when they meet you." Looking into her face was "just amazing because she's such a . . . a hero," Natalie told Rosie O'Donnell. "I mean, she risked her life to save these people, and she totally didn't have to."

Natalie was also touched by her tour of the home. All over Anne's walls were photographs of movie stars Anne had arranged with loving devotion. She had written her diary, in fact, in the belief that it would someday be published and perhaps made into a movie. Natalie understood that belief perfectly. Being a Jew did not mean that she couldn't have dreams of fame and fortune. One of Anne's final entries proclaimed, "I want to live on, even after death."

Even before she landed the role in the Broadway play, Natalie was fascinated by Anne Frank's story, especially since it was one to which her entire family could relate because of their losses in the Holocaust.

"We've been through so much—not me personally—but there are people who have sacrificed so much so I can be alive today," Natalie told author Jane Pratt. "My people in general have fought so hard that it gives me a sense of responsibility."

Besides the weight of that cultural responsibility, Natalie related to Anne as a teenager (Anne was not yet sixteen when she died) who coped with some of the same doubts and fears Natalie felt about becoming an adult. Wrote Anne, "I never utter my real feelings about anything . . . and [I] keep on trying to find a way of becoming what I would so like to be and what I could be if . . . there weren't any other people living in the world." Thoughts like that rang true for Natalie, as if she and Anne were soul mates traversing the same life circle.

* * *

The Diary of Anne Frank, written by Frances Goodrich and Albert Hackett and newly adapted by Wendy Kesselman, opened on December 4, 1997, at the Music Box Theatre at 239 West 45th Street in New York. The producers were optimistic about its potential for success because, in addition to Natalie, the cast included television veteran Linda Lavin, George Hearn, Harris Yulin, and Austen Pendleton.

Particularly optimistic was producer David Stone, who had initiated the project. At the preliminary reading, he told *Boston* magazine, "Natalie was so magnificent that not only was she crying during the last scene, but so were the other actors; their mouths were agape at this girl."

Not so optimistic was *Vanity Fair* writer Mimi Kramer, who wondered whether the producer's efforts to update the play would find a receptive

90

audience: "It's one of the season's most eagerly anticipated shows, but the question remains: Will . . . [it] seem old-fashioned when the new production . . . opens? The play hasn't exactly aged well."

The producers called it an adaptation because they'd asked writer Wendy Kesselman to choose new passages from the diary to highlight in the play, particularly those portions about Anne's emerging sexuality that her father had edited out of the original book, and to present Anne as more of a typical teenager with sometimes gyrating mood swings.

There is no question that Natalie considered it her most challenging role. In a preproduction interview with Bernard Hammelburg of the *New York Times*, she stressed the kinship she felt with Anne. "Her story is my own story," she said, sometimes shifting into Hebrew as she continued. "I grew up with the Holocaust. My grandparents came to Israel as sole survivors, having lost their entire families."

In an interview for *Harper's Bazaar* that took place while Natalie was still in London working on *Star Wars*, she met with writer Elizabeth Gleick in a swanky dining room at the Savoy Hotel. Gleick wanted to discuss both the movie and the play, but, like so many other interviewers who have confronted Natalie face to face, she was so taken by the actress that she put her best efforts into describing what she *saw* rather than what she heard as answers to her questions.

"This sweet sixteen-year-old actress may have played some of the oldest little girls that audiences have seen since Jodie Foster hit the big screen, but at the sight of the tiered silver tray bearing tiny little sandwiches and pristine pastries, Portman can barely contain a coltish excitement, and her big brown eyes grow to the size of scones," wrote Gleick. "In the space of about an hour, she manages to devour a couple of those, along with the better part of a pot of strawberry jam, any sandwiches that can remotely be classified as vegetarian and several pastries she emphatically pronounces 'the best.'"

The problem with Natalie playing Anne Frank was that by 1998 standards she was *bigger* than Anne. Natalie certainly did not feel that way, but her appearance in the play was greeted with layered tints of that perception.

During the course of the production, Natalie wrote personal essays for both *Time* and *Seventeen* magazines about the experience of doing the play. In a January 1998 cover story for *Seventeen*, Natalie wrote about how she felt playing Anne Frank. "This is the most honest book I've ever read because it is a true diary," she wrote. "It made me feel as if someone understood me. Anne Frank wrote about things that every teenager goes through but doesn't really discuss openly."

The *Seventeen* piece was thoughtful and well written, but it wasn't the editors' first choice. Originally, they wanted to interview Natalie about a wide range of topics, but she knew that the play would come up in the interview, and she didn't want it to be juxtaposed with a conversation about boys and makeup. It was her suggestion that she write the piece herself. The editors were respectful of the essay, but they did "glam" the story up a bit by going into detail elsewhere in the magazine about the makeup Natalie wore for the cover photograph (Instant Lash Mascara in black brown, cheek rouge in raspberry, and lipstick in Pink Sugar). Natalie did not seem to mind. Indeed, she knew that Anne would have understood perfectly.

The essay for *Time* magazine was published in the June 15, 1999, issue, a couple of months after the play ended its run. This piece was more thoughtful than the one Natalie had done for *Seventeen*, but it touched on some of the same teen themes that had drawn Natalie to the play:

adolescent angst, parental relationships, and confusing sexuality. "Anne's literal entrapment and terror figuratively describe the claustrophobia and fears of teenage experience," Natalie wrote. "Personally, she let me know that I was not weird when I was not getting along with adults, or was infatuated with a boy I knew I didn't really like."

Natalie began her media campaign to promote the play on November 24, 1997, with an appearance on *The Late Show with David Letterman*. As usual, she complained about the low temperature in the theater, saying that her fingers were, "like, falling off." Unique among talk-show hosts, Letterman likes to keep the theater temperature in the sixties, assuming that comedy, like a nice piece of meat, is best preserved at lower temperatures, a philosophy not always embraced by his guests.

Letterman asked Natalie how working on Broadway was different than making films.

"Well, you have to go through a lot more preparation for it," she said. "You have the whole rehearsal period. You have immediate response from the audience. And they've been training me for my vocal coaching, so that I can project more. They told me that I tend to slur my words, so I had to work with a person."

Letterman told her she was just fine, not to worry about it.

"You know, I've known you for a couple of years, and if somebody said 'Put together a list of your impressions about this young woman,' I don't think 'She slurs her words' would appear on that list."

"Thank you," said Natalie, laughing.

Her next television interview was in early December 1997 on *The Today Show*, where she was interviewed by Matt Lauer during the second hour of the show. Natalie told him that she had wanted to play Anne Frank ever since she'd read the book at the age of twelve.

Alluding to the changes in the play, Lauer asked her to explain how the audience might perceive the new version.

"Well, the Anne Frank that we've been presented with in the past has been this kind of saintly image of this young girl," she explained. "We wanted to present her as a real person. I mean, she was a very, very good person . . . but she was no saint."

Lauer reminded Natalie that her last visit had been in 1994 to talk about *The Professional*. He asked her how her life had changed since then. She told him that she still had the same friends, lived in the same house, and attended the same school.

After the holidays, Natalie finished up her television interviews on January 9, 1998, with an appearance on *The Rosie O'Donnell Show*. O'Donnell praised *The Diary of Anne Frank*, saying that she had seen it and had gone backstage after the play to talk to Natalie and costar Linda Lavin. "You know the story, and you know what's going to happen at the end, but it still rips your soul apart," said O'Donnell.

On the night O'Donnell attended, there was a man sitting nearby with his children. After the final curtain, while everyone in the audience was sitting in silence or sobbing, someone stood up and yelled at the man with the children, "You ruined this whole show for me. Your kids were talking so loud it ruined the whole show!"

O'Donnell was horrified at the man's behavior in allowing his children to talk, but was glad there were children in the audience. Natalie said that was sometimes the best part. She explained that children sometimes talk back to the actors and make silly noises, such as the kid who made a loud smoochy sound just as she was about to kiss one of her costars.

Reviews of the play were mixed—and for a variety of reasons. Some critics were incensed that the original script had been tampered with.

Others thought Natalie's experience as a movie star somehow made her less desirable for the stage role.

Ben Brantley of the *New York Times* had reservations about the play, but he had nothing but praise for Natalie. "To see Natalie Portman on the stage . . . is to understand what Proust meant when he spoke of girls in flower," he wrote. "Ms. Portman, a film actress making her Broadway debut, is only sixteen, and despite her precocious resume, she gives off a pure rosebud freshness that can't be faked. There is ineffable grace in her awkwardness, and her very skin seems to glow with the promise of miraculous transformations."

Everything that Brantley wrote was undoubtedly true, but it only served to point out the obvious: Natalie, budding superstar that she was, detracted from the theme of the play simply by being Natalie. That was never her intention, but that was the way it played out and was perhaps one reason why she asked for an early exit at the end of May 1998. Then, again, it may have been because she had other things to do.

* * *

Appearing in *The Diary of Anne Frank* was more demanding than Natalie had anticipated. During the day, she attended high school, which meant that, before her parents drove her into New York each evening to appear in the play, she had precious little time to study. Typically, she arrived at the theater early so she could study before the curtain call. Then after the play, when she was back home on Long Island, she studied again before going to bed.

But the stress of acting in the play was not all related to scheduling. The role of Anne Frank hit her hard emotionally. How could it not? But for the grace of God, she might have been Anne. Certainly, her family members had endured the same pain and suffering. Shortly before quitting the role,

Natalie admitted to the *New York Times* that it had been an emotionally draining experience. "One of the most painful things for me is that often, at the end of the show, I see a little kid in one of the front rows just crying uncontrollably. The more I lived with it every day, the more I realized there's no way I could feel what the real people felt."

Despite the long work hours, Natalie was able to maintain an A-plus average in school. Now finishing up her junior year, she began to think more about her future. "I don't know what I want to be," she told Patti Hartigan of the *Boston Globe*. "I love science, so maybe a doctor, I dunno. I love languages, so maybe a researcher." Then she threw up her arms and laughed. "Hey, maybe a farmer. Who knows?"

Of course, being a regular student was beyond Natalie's capacity for self-restraint. All the time she was enjoying the social and academic opportunities offered by the school, she was working on a writing project. It was not an essay about the Holocaust, nor was it one of those Oprah-like introspectives about finding her power as a woman. No, it was a scientific article titled "A Simple Method to Demonstrate the Enzymatic Production of Hydrogen from Sugar." Cowritten with Ian Hurley, who worked with her father at North Shore University Hospital, and Jonathan Woodward, who worked in the chemical technology division of the Oak Ridge National Laboratory at Oak Ridge, Tennessee, the article was based on her entry into the Intel Science Talent Search and offered a means by which the biodegradable content of municipal wastes could be converted to useful forms of energy.

The article, published in the October 1998 issue of the *Journal of Chemical Education*, offered an impressive amount of research into ways to convert wastes into alternative energy sources. Wrote Natalie, "It is shown that the renewable resource cellulose, in its soluble derivative from carboxymethylcellulose, as well as aspen-wood waste, is also a source of hydrogen if the enzyme cellulose is included in the reaction mixture."

Natalie took as many science classes as she could at Syosset High School, but she also took Japanese and French. Do you really have to decide what you want to do with the rest of your life at the age of seventeen? she wondered (she'd left sweet sixteen behind in April). Of course, most kids are asked that question only by their parents and relatives—and perhaps only a couple of times a year. Since Natalie was famous, she was asked that question nearly every time she did a media interview, which was often. It bothered her at times that she kept changing her mind about her life goals, but she good-naturedly attributed that to the fact she is a Gemini: "I change my mind every day."

"I don't know if I could live with acting my whole life because there are such huge periods between films," Natalie told Kristine McKenna for the *Los Angeles Times*. "I see these twenty-year-old actors who do nothing but smoke cigarettes and go to clubs every night while they wait for their next part, and I couldn't stand living that way . . . [but] I don't know if I could give it up. Acting is dangerous work because it's addictive."

Exhausted by her schedule—and cognizant of approaching tough decisions about college—Natalie put a hold on her interviews and acting for the remainder of her junior year.

*   *   *

By 1995, Hong Kong-born Wayne Wang had directed eight movies, but none of them, with the exception of 1993's *The Joy Luck Club*, had attracted a great deal of attention. Of Chinese heritage, he was known primarily as an ethnic filmmaker.

Wang's father was a devoted American movie fan, especially when it came to action and adventure films. When Wang was born, his father named him Wayne after his hero, John Wayne. With an upbringing like that, it's not surprising that Wang would look to movies as a possible career choice.

Wang studied film and television at California's College of Arts and Crafts, but when he returned to Hong Kong to find work in his chosen field he quickly discovered that it would take more than a degree. In the mid-1970s, he returned to the United States and settled in San Francisco, where he began his career in earnest. In 1975, he codirected a low-budget film titled *A Man, a Woman, and a Killer*, but it did nothing to enhance his career.

In 1981, Wang raised $22,000 in grants from the American Film Institute and the National Educational Association to produce his first film, *Chan Is Missing*. As you'd expect with a budget that size, Wang cowrote, directed, and produced the film. It attracted little attention, but his next project, *Dim Sum: A Little Bit of Heart*, established him as an up-and-coming director.

Wang was proud of his ethnic background, but he did not want to devote his life to making films about Chinese Americans. He wanted to explore the expanse of American cinema. He did not believe it was his destiny to remain an ethnic filmmaker; he had been named after John Wayne, not Charlie Chan.

In 1998, at the age of forty-nine, Wang was asked to be the director for *Anywhere but Here*, a mother-daughter story based on a book by Mona Simpson. It was exactly the type of story he had been looking for, one that allowed for creative license but had a broad enough theme to appeal to a mainstream audience.

Susan Sarandon was the perfect actress to play the role of the mother. She had played various roles in her career, but the parts that always brought her the most attention were those in which she played opposite one or more women. Perhaps the role with which she is most closely associated is the one in *Thelma and Louise* (1991), a groundbreaking film in which she played opposite Geena Davis.

Another movie in which Sarandon displayed feminine resonance was *Witches of Eastwick* (1987). Although Jack Nicholson was the male lead and has always inspired good performances from female costars, Sarandon's best energies came from her interactions with Cher and Michelle Pfeiffer.

Of all the movies Sarandon made before signing on to work with Wang, it was probably her role in 1978's *Pretty Baby* that made him think she was perfect for the part in *Anywhere but Here*. In *Pretty Baby*, she played the mother of a twelve-year-old girl who lived with her in a bordello. Sarandon delivered a spellbinding performance while interacting with the other prostitutes, but it was her screen rapport with her daughter, played by Brooke Shields, that was memorable.

Pretty Baby, directed by French filmmaker Louis Malle, attracted controversy in 1978, not only because Sarandon appeared nude, but also because Shields, who was filmed without her shirt, portrayed a character that became a prostitute at the tender age of twelve. The film was released at a time when state and federal lawmakers were trying to enact legislation to restrict the activities of child pornographers. Malle, Sarandon (who was romantically involved with the director at the time), and Shields came under attack because of the content of the film.

"My God, this strange impulse of man's being sexually aroused by children has been part of every civilization," Malle told *Playboy* magazine in defense of the movie. "That's a fact, I'm sorry to say, a sociological fact—and it's going on today, in New York City, in the so-called

99

Minnesota Strip on Eighth Avenue, which is nothing but kids whoring. Let me make clear that I'm a film maker, not a social worker."

Reaction to the film was so strong that a child-welfare group threatened to take Shields out of her mother's custody. Shields and her mother eventually went on television together to tell their side of the story. Shields denied that her mother and Malle had abused her by putting her in the film. There was nothing sexy about her part, she said.

The uproar made the movie an instant box-office success, and reviewers proclaimed Shields to be a star on the rise. "Move over, Tatum," said *Playboy.* "Make way, Jodie. Brooke is here, and from the look of things she could be a Wunderkind to beat all."

Pretty Baby was about a twelve-year-old girl who lost her virginity in a whorehouse filled with emotionally needy women whose view of life was so self-centered that they could not relate to the needs of a child who was becoming a woman. *Anywhere but Here* was about a mother facing similar emotional conflicts. Since the script called for Sarandon's daughter to lose her virginity at a time when the mother was giving away sex in an effort to find emotional comfort, who could possibly play the daughter better than cinema's current Wunderkind, Natalie Portman?

To Wang, it was a match made in heaven. There had been magic between Sarandon and Shields in 1978, so why couldn't it be re-created in 1998 with Sarandon and Portman? It was a grand vision with only one flaw: Brooke's mother and Natalie's mother were poles apart when it came to on-screen sexuality.

Wang sent the script to Natalie for her consideration and awaited her reply. When he received word that she was ready to discuss it, he suggested they do so over dinner. Natalie was happy to oblige. She told Wang that she and her parents thought the script was wonderful, but they had problems with the scene in which the daughter loses her virginity. The scene called for nudity, and Natalie and her parents thought that wasn't right for her as an actress. She told him she had too much respect for his vision as a director to ask him to change it. Thanks, but no thanks.

Natalie's rejection of the script was a setback for Wang, but it would only get worse for the director. When he informed Sarandon that Natalie had declined, Sarandon was blunt: no Natalie, no Susan.

"Everything was at a standstill—I was very upset," Wang told Leslie Bennetts of *Vanity Fair.* "Sometimes I think Natalie's parents were over protective, but if I look at it from their point of view, in this industry you almost need to overcompensate, and maybe that's good. If I had a daughter like Natalie, I would probably do exactly what her parents are doing."

Wang huddled with screenwriter Alvin Sargent, and they decided that the nude scene could be deleted without damaging the script. When Wang notified Natalie of the change and asked her to reconsider, she readily accepted.

* * *

Anywhere but Here begins with Natalie and Sarandon on the road in a Mercedes-Benz. In a way, it is *Thelma and Louise* all over again, except that Natalie plays the role of an anti-Thelma. Natalie's character hates the way her mother talks, she hates the music her mother listens to on the radio, and she hates the fact that her mother has snatched her out of a comfortable home to go to Beverly Hills in search of an elusive dream. The last thing in the world that she wants is to be her mother's "buddy."

"This is like being kidnapped," Natalie complains. "You don't understand that, do you?"

"I wish somebody had kidnapped me when I was your age."

"So do I," says a stone-faced Natalie.

101

She is upset because her mother has left her stepfather and taken her on the road to California. Emotionally, the two are on the same highway, only going in different directions. Natalie is groping to find herself as an adolescent, while her mother is trying to find herself as an unhappy post-adolescent.

Once they relocate in Beverly Hills—and Sarandon finds a job as a schoolteacher—Natalie tries to come to terms with the realization that, as much as she loves her mother, they are totally different people. Natalie dreams of the day when she can leave home to find her own happiness.

Anywhere but Here was the first movie since *The Professional* in which Natalie had a strong costarring role, and she threw herself into it totally. The chemistry between Sarandon and Natalie was everything Wang hoped it would be. There are any number of good scenes in the movie, but one of the best occurs when Sarandon forces Natalie to audition for a movie role. While Natalie is improvising her audition, Sarandon quietly opens the door to eavesdrop. To her horror, Natalie repeats their mother-daughter conversations in a way that is unflattering to Sarandon. It is an emotional scene because it goes to the core of their dysfunctional relationship.

"Beverly Hills—what a bummer," Natalie says in concluding her audition. "But . . . so what? Like my daddy used to always say . . . [she breaks into song, singing 'Be optimistic and smile . . .']."

Realizing the truth about their relationship, Sarandon flees the room, eventually to come to terms with her worst nightmare, that Natalie will someday leave her alone with her broken dreams.

Natalie herself had given a lot of thought in recent months to leaving home. At times, she thought the movie applied to her own life. "I actually thought I had felt a lot of the things before, because you always have conflicts with your mom growing up," she told James Lapine for *Interview* magazine. "My mom and I have a much more together relationship than the mother and daughter in the movie, though."

When *Anywhere but Here* was released in November 1999, critics were enthusiastic about Natalie's performance. Wrote Edward Guthmann in the *San Francisco Chronicle*, "Portman seems to draw from some creative well that most actors only dream of. . . . [S]he raises the bar for other actresses, and she almost upstages her formidable co-star, Susan Sarandon." Roger Ebert wrote in the *Chicago Sun-Times* that the performances, not the plot, set the tone of the movie: "Sarandon's role is trickier and more difficult, but Portman's will get the attention. . . . [H]er best scenes are when she fights back, not emotionally, but with incisive observations."

Natalie was nominated for a Golden Globe award for her role in the movie, and, even though she did not win, it was a significant marker in her career. Also heaping praise on her was her costar, who told the *San Jose Mercury News* that she would not be surprised by anything Natalie does in the future.

"There are a lot of good actresses her age, but she has this core of dignity, health, grace and innate intelligence that's a pretty formidable package when you put it all together."

*   *   *

When Natalie started school in the fall of 1999, she was a senior. She could hardly believe it. During her first three years of high school, she had appeared in five movies and a Broadway play—was that insane or what?— yet she had carried on as a normal student with normal problems, fears, and expectations. The only thing that really set her apart was that, unlike most of the other students her age, she still did not have a driver's license and was driven to school each morning by her mother.

103

With one year of high school left, Natalie was thinking more and more about college. Where should she go? What should she study? Should she continue to make movies in the summer months or give acting up entirely until she graduated from college? She had signed a contract to star in two additional *Star Wars* movies, but she could eliminate everything else. She could become a regular girl.

The first big school event of the year was Spirit Week, held each year from September 28 to October 2. Designed to pump up the spirits of Syosset High School's football team, the Braves, it was a time when students were allowed to go crazy at school. The week began with Pajama Day, when students were allowed to wear pajamas or other "crazy" clothing to school, and ended with the cheerleaders leading a massive pep rally the day before the big game. All of the students, including Natalie, painted their faces with the school colors of red, black, and white, and some donned headbands decorated with feathers. It was sort of like being in a *Star Wars* movie, only without the million-dollar paycheck.

The following day at the big game, students wore the same painted faces and Indian headgear. Shortly after the kickoff, Syosset students were stunned when the opponents, the Plainview Hawks, put a quick seven points on the scoreboard. But the Hawks didn't know what they were up against. The Braves went on to score three touchdowns, winning 21-7.

In December, Natalie expanded her scientific profile by participating in a program aired by National Public Radio. Titled *Gray Matter: The Teenage Brain*, the one-hour documentary was sponsored by the Dana Foundation, a private philanthropic organization. Natalie served as the moderator for the program, which talked about depression, suicide, and sleep problems among adolescents.

"Adolescence can be an extraordinarily difficult time for young people, but it's worth remembering . . . that most kids get through their teenage years rather smoothly," Natalie said. "In fact, they thrive. While tremendous challenges mark the passage to adulthood, scientists have found that the teenage brain . . . usually copes with the onslaught of emotions and physical growth just fine and that perhaps with respect to adolescence that is the most amazing thing of all."

Only seventeen, Natalie had appeared in six movies and a Broadway play, and she had written articles on serious subjects for *Time*, *Seventeen*, and the *Journal of Chemical Education*. She could speak Hebrew, Japanese, and French, and she could dance on top of a chair without falling off. What university would not be delighted to enroll the brown-eyed goddess in any course of study she chose?

Chapter 5

Finally Coming of Age

Sex was problematic for Natalie Portman. It created difficulties for her without dispensing any benefits. It had been that way almost from the beginning of her career. By playing the role of Mathilda in *The Professional*, she'd opened the door to sexual interpretations of her subsequent characters and her personal life.

Because of the roles Natalie played, people often responded to her as if she were a sexually precocious child. Nothing could have been further from the truth. She talked about the issue to anyone who would listen, saying time and time again that Mathilda's love for Leon in *The Professional* wasn't sexual and that Marty's relationship with Willie in *Beautiful Girls* was a promise of things to come and not the reality of the moment.

Yet everyone it seemed wanted her to be the hell-bound sex child, wink-wink, they perceived in the movies. And it wasn't just pedophiles harboring thos3e thoughts—it was everyone!

All of which gave Natalie the creeps.

That may have been one reason Natalie reacted so strongly when she was offered the title role in Adrian Lyne's 1997 adaptation of *Lolita*. She was incensed that he would even offer the role to her, as if it were an insult.

"Let me tell you, this movie's going to be sleaze," she told the *New York Times*. "He [Lyne] did *9 ½ Weeks* and *Indecent Proposal*. Oh, that was a real quality movie."

Natalie's mother tried to soften her daughter's words by explaining to the newspaper that she did not want Natalie to have a sexual scene at the age of thirteen (when the part was offered), portraying feelings that she may not "experience in life until she's seventeen."

"I just don't think there needs to be a film about a thirteen-year-old girl having intercourse with a fifty-year-old man," Natalie explained on *Good Morning America*. "It's just not something that I think we need in society right now."

Natalie did not have a problem with sex. Her problem was with the sex-child mold she'd fallen into at such an early age. On the subject of sex in general, she was much more analytical. "People my age have a lot of sexuality," the fourteen year old told *Sassy* magazine. "It's a mixture of your hormones just beginning and everything you see around you—TV, movies, whatever. If we were living in a bubble, we wouldn't know what to do with hormones—we'd probably just be eating a lot or something!— but when you see this stuff around, you go, 'Oh, so that's what hormones are for!'"

In 1999, as Natalie went from seventeen to eighteen, it was fairly obvious that her mother's assumption that she would have had a sexual experience by then was wrong. There were probably a lot of reasons for that. Even if Natalie had been willing, can you imagine the mental and emotional contortions that a sixteen- or seventeen-year-old boy would have to go through to make a pass at the girl who played Mathilda and Marty? It is tough enough when the girls are simply classmates, but when they are also movie stars, forget it!

During this time, Natalie often wondered aloud to reporters why so many older men, rather than boys her own age, were interested in her. She may have been a movie star, but celebrity didn't seem to bring her opportunities to end her celibacy with boys. Certainly, she had male friends and took escorts to school functions—and sometimes she had crushes on boys in her school—but there was no love of her life in the picture. How depressing was that?

On top of the logistics of finding romance were the doubts Natalie had about her own development. At eighteen, she wasn't much taller than she'd been at fourteen. She was self-conscious about being five-feet-two. She imagined that her fans expected her to be taller. Her hips were wider than she wanted them to be. She had dark eyes and dark hair, characteristics not often associated with stardom. "I'm not that average blond-haired, blue-eyed American girl," she once lamented to author Jane Pratt.

In short, despite international fame, adolescence was a living hell for Natalie. What she needed at this point in her life was a symbol of victory. Some signs of encouragement, however faint, that would boost her self-image.

What she got instead was her worst nightmare.

At eighteen, while Natalie was still being driven to school by her mother, and not yet decided about what being eighteen really meant, her old nemesis from *Ruthless* reared her newly tinted blonde head and rocked Natalie's world. In 1999, at the age of seventeen (Natalie is eight months older than Britney Spears), the teen singer rocked pop music with a debut album titled *Baby One More Time*. Although adult magazines such as *People* were critical of Britney—she is "peppy and enthusiastic" but not "precocious enough"—young music buyers liked the album enough to make it a best-seller, with sales eventually reaching the ten-million mark.

Britney became an overnight phenomenon. A big part of her early success was the image she projected of a young, Lolita-like schoolgirl. Her first video, which featured the title song, showed her in schoolgirl clothing

108

with a bare midriff and displayed a hormone-thumping attitude that seemed to scream out for attention. Was this the same girl who had made funny faces during performances of *Ruthless*? With one album, Britney had done what it had taken Natalie several movies to do: she had become a teen sex queen. Like Natalie, Britney said it was all an image, just like the Lolitaesque cover she did for *Rolling Stone* magazine.

"What's the big deal?" she told *US* magazine. "I have really strong morals, and just because I look sexy on the cover of *Rolling Stone* doesn't mean I'm a naughty girl."

Also like Natalie, Britney appealed to older males, most of whom should have known better but didn't because Britney seemed to be so willingly accessible to their fantasies. "I've been finding that there are a lot of older guys in the audience lately," she confessed to *Rolling Stone* in 2000, about a year after the release of her first album. "The other night we had a show, and I was walking around before I go off, and this guy jumps up on the stage, takes his shirt off and comes running. I think the crowd thought it was supposed to happen, but security jumped on the stage and got him off."

When Natalie flirted with older men, it was like a private joke. Britney flirted with *everyone*—men of all ages, women, and children—and in a very public way. Will anyone ever forget her Pepsi commercial in which former presidential candidate Bob Dole who hadn't been fifty in over two decades, saw the singer performing on television and admonished his dog "Down boy!"?

Britney was giving closet Lolitas a bad name and, at the same time, forcing Natalie to make some serious decisions about herself. Britney said all the same things about herself that Natalie said—namely, that she was moral, chaste, and loving of her family—and there was no reason to question the singer's veracity. Yet Britney was using underage sex appeal to successfully further her career, and she was doing it without a second thought, at least not publicly.

When Natalie looked at Britney, she saw someone who had the same doubts and insecurities but did something about them. Her normally mousy hair had exploded into a blonde firestorm reminiscent of Marilyn Monroe. And, perhaps most intriguing of all to Natalie, Britney flaunted her emerging sexuality on stage, all the while denying that it was the "real" her.

Natalie viewed Britney as her nemesis not because the singer had done something bad to her—she hadn't—but because she had pushed the envelope for stardom. Natalie was too old now to play Lolita roles, too old to be the little girl with an old soul, but she was the same age as Britney, and what she saw in the singer's career was a mirror image of what she knew studio executives and moviegoers would expect from her in the future.

Natalie was an experienced dancer and stage performer. She could wow audiences with her bare midriff if she wanted to, she could gyrate with the best of them (she'd done that since the age of three), but did she really want to do that? Was it possible to have a movie career as an adult woman without succumbing to the sexual stereotypes of young leading ladies? The very thought of being nude in a movie or on stage horrified Natalie. Some actresses have forged solid movie careers without nudity—Julia Roberts is perhaps the best example—but Natalie understood that such careers are rare.

What also frustrated the intellectual side of Natalie was that stardom is all about public perception. Britney had controlled her image to the point that, if fans ever questioned whether she'd take her top off on stage, the answer would be . . . of course! The fact that her fans would think that, despite the singer's pledges to family, God, and country, is the reason that Britney would never have to take her top off.

On the other hand, if Natalie's fans were asked the same question, the answer would overwhelmingly be . . . of course not! That was why Natalie would have to take her top off—to prove her credibility as an adult actress. Because no one would ever believe she would do it. Ironically, the family pressures on Natalie, as the only child of Jewish parents, were almost identical to the pressures placed on Britney by her parents, products of the Deep South. Southern girls and Northern Jewish girls are more alike than they are different, and if you put them in the same room they will not stop talking to each other about their parents.

Mental games ordinarily delighted Natalie, but this one about Britney was not so much a game as it was her life and future as an actress. Besides, this was her last semester of high school. Mostly, she wanted to think about more mundane issues such as boys, perhaps the only subject she did not fully understand!

Asked by *Jane* magazine that year what she would name as the three qualities she looks for in a boyfriend, Natalie responded: "Being able to talk about anything. I love reading books with friends and talking about them. People who cry over poetry—it sounds stupid, but it's so nice to be with someone who can be moved by art." Asked for two more qualities, she said, "someone who is smart and who . . . will show me new things" and someone with a good sense of humor, though she's not attracted to, "like, a comedian."

One other bit of advice for would-be suitors: one phone call per day is your limit. More than one call and you risk being labeled creepy. And if you are thinking about calling but have nothing really important to say, then your time will be better spent playing a video game, because Natalie has a thing about dead airtime.

*   *   *

From January until early May 1999, Natalie put her career aside, except for an appearance on *The Rosie O'Donnell Show* and an interview for *Vanity Fair*, so she could focus on her studies. Of course, they weren't always drudgery. That spring her Japanese class traveled to Japan. Natalie and her classmates took Hershey Kisses with them to hand out as gifts to people they encountered, a gesture that was met with widespread approval. Teenagers being teenagers, they then persuaded their newfound friends to pose in photographs with them, their cheeks usually bulging with chocolate candy.

One of the highlights of the trip was a visit to a Buddhist temple, where they watched worshipers meditate in the lotus position. Whenever a worshiper placed his or her palms together, indicating that a spiritual connection had been made, a monk would appear and whack them with a branch, sending them back into meditation. Natalie and her classmates assumed the position to mimic the worshipers, but they were not too keen on getting whacked, so it was only when the monk complained that he wasn't getting to whack them that they went along with the routine and took their whacking like good Buddhists.

Natalie liked Japan, especially the part about not hugging or kissing. The Japanese bowed instead of shaking hands or hugging, she reasoned, because they did not want to catch germs. That was cool with her.

When the class returned to New York, Natalie took care of a little unfinished business. Since she would be going to college in the fall, she decided it was time to get her driver's license. She was late signing up for the driver's education class at school, so she was not accepted. Instead, she enrolled in a private driver's ed school.

When Natalie took her driver's examination, it did not go exactly as planned. During one of her turns, she accidentally switched on the windshield wipers and in the confusion hit the brakes, stopping in the middle of the intersection. The instructor gave her another opportunity to make a left turn, but she flubbed it as well, turning in front of the oncoming traffic. Despite her difficulties—test examiners see much worse in an average day—she was approved for a driver's license. Now Natalie was a legal driver. In another few weeks, she would be nineteen—and legal in every sense of the word.

Early in the year, Leslie Bennetts, a writer for *Vanity Fair*, visited Natalie at Syosset High School (with her parents' permission, of course, and with the understanding that her real name would not be used) to hang out with the teen queen while she went about her duties as a high school student.

"In person, Portman has an indisputable lovely face, but she's not really a head turner," wrote Bennetts. "Put her in front of a camera, however, and that face will break your heart."

Bennetts noticed that when Natalie changed classes she stayed close to the wall to avoid the student rush, looking younger than her classmates and as "fragile as an orchid." During one class, she snacked on a peanut butter sandwich.

When Natalie met her friends in the cafeteria, they all wanted to talk about the upcoming senior prom. Natalie was enthusiastic about the prom, but since she didn't have a boyfriend she was wondered if she should go alone.

"Boys want to go to the prom with someone they can fool around with," she said—and that clearly wouldn't be her. Perhaps afraid that Bennetts would think she was too much of a goody-goody, she explained her feelings about differences between herself and some of her peers. "I would never say someone else is bad because they do something, but for myself, I'm kind of conservative," she said. "I've never tried smoking, I don't drink, I've never tried any drugs. I don't condemn people who do; I've just never wanted to."

Photofest

Chapter 6

Star Wars as a Way of Life

Natalie would happily have gone all the way to graduation without another intrusion of her professional life into her student life, but that was just not in the cards for her, not when she was starring in the biggest movie of the year.

Star Wars: The Phantom Menace was released on May 21, 1999. For months, the publicity machine had been churning out prerelease products, the most ubiquitous being Diet Pepsi cans and advertisements with Natalie's image as Queen Amidala prominently displayed. On the day of the movie's release, Natalie appeared on *The Late Show with David Letterman*. She had appeared on his show five times, more than on any other talk show on television, and despite his unpredictability as a host she clearly felt at ease with him. She especially liked playing grownup to his naughty boy. It always made her laugh. In fact, no one on television could make her laugh the way Dave did.

Letterman mentioned the *Star Wars* movie when he introduced Natalie, but he did not bring it up again until the end of the interview, when he congratulated her on the *Star Wars* blockbuster. Publicists for the movie must have been unhappy, since that movie was the reason she'd been booked on the show. But she didn't seem to mind at all.

Mostly, Letterman asked Natalie about her personal life. She told him about the trip to Japan and about getting her driver's license. He especially enjoyed talking to her about the license. One of the evening's funniest segments occurred when he gave her a hypothetical test question. If four drivers arrived at a four-way stop at the same time, he asked, who had the right-of-way?

"The first person that gets to the stop," Natalie answered.

No, no, Letterman protested. He said the car with the right-of-way was the car to the right.

Natalie stuck to her guns, never losing patience with him. Finally, she explained that everyone at the intersection would be to the right of *someone*.

"Ah," Letterman said, seeing the light. "It's the car to the right or the car that arrived there first."

"Thank you," said Natalie triumphantly.

In the end, it didn't matter whether or not Natalie talked about *Star Wars* on the Letterman show. There was so much publicity for the movie that everyone already knew about her starring role in it. About a week before the official release, *Star Wars* fans sneaked into advance screenings and then posted their comments on the Internet.

The early Internet buzz on the movie seemed to fall into one of two categories: hard-core fans voiced disappointment, and new fans seemed to be uninterested. The consensus was that, while it was a good movie, it did not live up to the hype that had preceded it.

Following in the wake of the Internet reviewers were the professional critics. Richard Corliss, writing in *Time* magazine, thought the dialogue was "way too starchy." To him, director George Lucas had put more emphasis on the art direction than on the actors. He thought Natalie's line readings are often "flat or flat-out wrong." In conclusion, he wrote that *The Phantom Menace* is "A phantom movie, the merest hint of a terrific saga that the final two episodes of the new trilogy may reveal."

Roger Ebert of the *Chicago Sun-Times* put the movie in perspective. How quickly everyone has forgotten the visionary magic of the first *Star Wars* series, he observed, and then he pointed out the obvious. "At the risk of offending devotees of the Force, I will say that the stories of the *Star Wars* movies have always been space operas, and that the importance of the movies comes from their energy, their sense of fun, their colorful inventions and their state-of-the-art special effects," he wrote. "I do not attend with the hope of gaining insights into human behavior."

Perhaps because the debate over whether the movie had lived up to expectations never affected its box-office appeal—it took in $240 million in the first eight weeks—Natalie seemed to be unconcerned about the critics.

"I didn't really mind," she told *E! Online*. "I thought it accomplished what it set out to accomplish, and I know a lot of kids who liked it. The intended audience got it. Sometimes reviewers are right, and sometimes they can be hideously wrong."

Natalie found a better reception in London, where the film was given a royal premiere at the Odeon Theatre on Leicester Square. "It is unbelievable here," she told a reporter from the *Telegraph*. "We never get this much excitement at a premiere in the States."

Interviewed for British television in the lobby of a London hotel, Natalie admitted that she'd had no idea how the movie would turn out because all the special effects had been added later. "We literally shot things in a parking lot with a blue sheet behind us, and, all of a sudden, in the film it is this magnificent castle with trees," she said. "It looks so real, and it looks like I'm actually there. It's bizarre because I know I've never been there, but I'm seeing it on a screen, so it's really a strange feeling."

Also strange were the promotional efforts that linked the film with certain products. She spotted herself on Kentucky Fried Chicken boxes, even though she is a vegetarian. It made no sense to her.

Natalie told *Empire* magazine that the movie had changed her life but not as much as she'd feared. "I can still pretty much lead a normal life," she said. "It was good that I had a career before *Star Wars* and that is not the only way I am defined. But it has definitely increased my recognisability."

*   *   *

Coupled with the *Star Wars* release was Natalie's high school graduation, an event that equaled, at least for the actress, the zany hoopla associated with the film. To her surprise, some of her classmates offered their yearbooks, which contained photographs of Natalie along with her real name, for auction on eBay and other Internet auction sites. In addition to her senior portrait, the yearbook shows photographs of Natalie as a child, on the track team, and, perhaps best of all, the student "most likely to appear on *Jeopardy*." The yearbooks sold for nearly six hundred dollars each, much more than the yearbooks of Connie Chung and Shirley MacLaine.

By the time prom night rolled around, Natalie had changed her mind about going to it alone. She went with a neighborhood boy she had known since she first moved to Long Island. Along with Natalie's other friends, they piled into a sixteen-seat Hummer limousine and made the hour-long trip to Manhattan, where they said good-bye to their childhood at a party in the Waldorf-Astoria Hotel. It sometimes bothered Natalie that she did not have a boyfriend, indeed had never even been in love, but on that night all she could think about was having a good time. And she did, dancing the night away with a ferociousness that at times seemed to be born of some inner desperation.

Natalie was graduating not only from her high school but also from the secure protection of her family. "I think moving out of the house is going to have a much bigger impact on me than this movie [*The Phantom Menace*]," she told *Premiere*. The prospect excited her and frightened her at the same time. Would she be free at last? Or would she become a slave to her past?

The following day, Natalie and 435 other seniors showed up at Syosset High School for commencement. Also there was a rowdy assemblage of national news media representatives, there to cover the graduation of Queen Amidala.

If people expected Natalie to be dressed in a queen's regalia, then they were surely disappointed because she blended in with all the other white-robed students who had gathered for the commencement ceremonies. Superintendent Carole Hankin pointed out to the audience that ninety-eight percent of the graduates would continue their education in college, "one of the highest averages in the country."

Michael Ma, who along with Natalie had been chosen the most likely student to appear on *Jeopardy*, was the valedictorian. Salutatorian Robert Wong, quoting New York Yankees legend Yogi Berra, might well have been speaking for Natalie when he said, "If you don't know where you're going, you'll end up someplace else."

Although the superintendent did not say so, among the students headed for college was Natalie Portman, who'd been accepted at Harvard University. But unlike the other college-bound graduates, she had a motion picture to make before she could call herself a college freshman.

*   *   *

120

For years, Austin, Texas, has been known for edgy country music, blue-eyed electric blues, and old-fashioned, three-chord rock 'n' roll, but recently the city has also acquired a reputation as a filmmaking mecca. Austin-made films such as *Spy Kids*, *The Getaway*, *The Great Waldo Pepper*, and *Miss Congeniality* have given the city an international reputation. In 2000, filmmakers did $120 million worth of business with the city, according to Brenda Johnson of the Austin Film Office, and that's hardly chump change.

In June 2000, Natalie flew into Austin from New York and checked into the Four Seasons Hotel. She had never been to Texas, so she did not know exactly what to expect. The first thing she noticed was that it was hot, with the temperature already in the mid-nineties. If it ever got that hot on Long Island in June, then the air would have been filled with urgent pleas for emergency assistance. Asked about the heat, Texans had only one comment: "You ain't seen nothing yet."

Natalie went to Austin to film *Where the Heart Is*, a story about a seventeen-year-old, pregnant, Tennessee girl, Novalee Nation, who has some uncommon experiences in Oklahoma after setting out for California with her boyfriend. Costarring in the film with Natalie were Ashley Judd, Stockard Channing, James Frain, and Sally Field. Matt Williams II, a veteran television producer and writer—*Roseanne*, *Home Improvement*, and *Thunder Alley*—was a virgin when it came to directing movies. *Where the Heart Is* was his first.

Cocooned in the heavily air-conditioned Four Seasons Hotel, Natalie must have thought she was in for an easy ride. That line of thinking changed abruptly when she learned that she would not actually be filming in Austin. As it turns out, most of the films that Austin takes credit for are shot in small towns and cities within a thirty-mile radius of the city. On the screen, *Where the Heart Is* takes place in Sequoyah, Oklahoma, but it was filmed in Round Rock, about twenty miles north of Austin, and in Lockhart, about thirty miles south of Austin. That meant that Natalie and her costars had to be bused each day of filming, catapulted from the pleasant environment of the Four Seasons Hotel, where they were pampered by the service staff and protected by the public relations staff, into the stark reality of small-town life. For Natalie, that also meant stepping from Beverly Hills, the site of her last filming, into the streets of *Lonesome Dove*. As you might expect from a girl of good breeding, Natalie thought all that was pretty damn cool, even if the sizzling sun threatened to blister her porcelain skin.

Since the plot of *Where the Heart Is* revolves around two different Wal-Mart stores, location scouts had to find communities that had already been Wal-Marted. Luckily, both Lockhart and Round Rock have Wal-Mart stores.

In years past, Round Rock and Lockhart were best known for their contributions to the Chisholm Trail, a path used by cattle ranchers to move their cattle herds north through Abilene into Kansas and beyond. In fact, the first herd to be placed on the Chisholm Trail originated in Lockhart.

Today Round Rock, with a population of sixty thousand, and Lockhart, with a population of twelve thousand, are best known for the ways in which they have adapted to contemporary life. Round Rock is the home of Dell Computer Corporation and the Round Rock Express, an AA minor league baseball franchise affiliated with the Houston Astros. Lockhart advertises itself as the "Barbecue Capital of Texas," thanks in part to the Texas Legislature, which passed a resolution granting the city that distinction, and as the filmmaking center of Texas. The Lockhart Chamber of Commerce listed on its website the titles of twenty-eight movies made in and around the city, including *Texas Justice*, *Tornado*, and *Honeysuckle Rose*. Today that number has swelled to thirty-three films.

"One of the reasons the film industry likes to come here is because they can film with relative ease," maintains Lockhart mayor Ray Sanders. "We make it easy for them to do so. The townspeople who do go out and watch the film [being made] are not intrusive."

Lockhart also attracts attention because of its old-fashioned courthouse and sleepy town square. Filmmakers use them to represent a modern throwback to another era or a premodern, wild-west era. Williams used the square in several scenes in *Where the Heart Is*. Said Mayor Sanders, "I went down and watched a couple of shootings . . . and I was amazed to see how they converted, in July, part of the square into a Christmas tree lot, and how they made the snow on the ground with cotton, and [how they] wet down the streets to get the reflection while they were shooting. It was just amazing. It was Christmas in July in Lockhart."

One of the extras in the Christmas tree scene was Beverly Annas, employed as a second grade teacher when she isn't working as a movie extra. The forty-nine-year-old mother of two daughters, both of whom have worked as movie extras, has been in eight movies, including *Tornado*, *Deadly Family Secrets*, and *She Fought Alone*.

When Annas first heard that *Where the Heart Is* would be filmed in Lockhart, she had to ask around about Natalie Portman because she had never heard of her. "Then someone said, 'Oh, she was in *Star Wars*,'" recalled Annas. "The only time I was close to her was in the grocery store, because we were standing at one of the checkout lines. I didn't talk to her. They tell us not to talk to the stars. I thought she was cute."

None of the stars interacted with the extras, but that didn't concern Annas. She figured they were trying to get into the mind-sets for their scenes and needed privacy to bridge that gap between reality and fantasy.

"One of the reasons I enjoy being an extra," Annas explained, "is because I find all the behind-the-scenes stuff very interesting. I could just sit for hours and watch them set up scenes." One of the scenes in *Where the Heart Is* that caught her eye is the one in which Natalie is inside a Wal-Mart store giving birth to a baby. Moviegoers see cascading sheets of rain against the store's windows; Annas saw a big water truck spraying water against the windows.

In addition to being in the Christmas tree lot scene, Annas was in a Wal-Mart scene in which Natalie examines clothing in the baby department ("I was one of the extras browsing through the clothes") and in a grocery store scene cut from the final print. The Wal-Mart scene took about seven hours to complete, Annas recalled. "There was a lot of sitting and waiting," she said. "They get you there, and they set up the scene and rehearse." During the downtime in Wal-Mart, Natalie and Ashley stood together and talked for a while; then Ashley picked up a magazine and started thumbing through it, looking much like a real-life shopper standing in the checkout line.

Natalie kept to herself and talked mostly to Ashley, said Annas. "She didn't really talk to any of the extras. She wasn't rude or anything. She stood around for a while, and then walked off somewhere, and [later] they called her back in."

For Lockhart, it was just another day. The residents were used to seeing film crews on the square and big vans and trailers at the city's only Catholic church. "They tend to use the churches," explained Annas, "because they have the big fellowship halls where they can feed everyone,

124

and they have the big parking lots where they can put their trailers." Trying to be ecumenical, Williams turned to the Presbyterian church when he needed a manger for the movie's emotional kidnap scene. The more he could spread around publicity for the churches, the better for all involved.

Public acceptance of the film crews is one reason why movie companies keep returning to the city, says Mayor Sanders. "Usually, when the stars come down, it's not like a big-city premiere. Most of the folks here like to glance at them, but they don't interfere in any way. They can come here and relax and not be harassed. The people in town respect what they do."

The only complaint that the mayor and the townspeople have about the whole thing is Austin's propensity for taking all the credit. "It kinda' grates a little when you look at the film credits and it says Austin instead of Lockhart," said Sanders. "Yeah, that grates us a little, but not enough that we are going to worry about it. We'd rather have them come here. . . . [I]t's an economic thing for us."

*   *   *

Where the Heart Is was an adventure for Natalie in more ways than one. It was the first film in which she was expected to carry most of the scenes. She had *stolen* (not intentionally, of course) scenes in *The Professional* and *Anywhere but Here*, but that had been because of her on-screen persona and not because the scripts had called for it. *Where the Heart Is* put Natalie in the driver's seat from the get-go.

Fortunately, she was backed up by costars who knew the territory, the most important of whom was thirty-two-year-old Ashley Judd. The daughter of Naomi Judd and the sister of Wynona Judd, she'd raced across cinematic skies like a comet since landing a role in 1991 in the critically acclaimed television series *Sisters*. By 2000, she had appeared in nearly two dozen films, including *Ruby in Paradise* (1993), *A Time to Kill* (1996), and *Double Jeopardy* (1999).

Natalie and Ashley had worked together in *Heat*, but they'd done no scenes together. Casting Ashley opposite Natalie was risky for the director because there was a possibility that the Kentucky-raised daughter of country music royalty would outshine Natalie, who had to do more than act in the movie; she had to assume a Southern accent and pass herself off as trailer-park white trash, a peculiar breed that she'd never encountered while growing up on Long Island.

The gamble paid off because Natalie did her homework, though her Southern accent was a little creaky at times, and because Ashley wisely pulled back when she could have overshadowed Natalie on the Southern drawl *thang*. Ashley does not have a Southern drawl at this point in her life, but she certainly knows how to re-create it with rapturous glee whenever called on to do so.

Like everyone else associated with the movie, Ashley was respectful of Natalie's emerging talent. When Jeff Jensen, a reporter from *Entertainment Weekly*, interviewed Natalie for a cover story, he also talked to Ashley about Natalie.

"It's hot here," Ashley cracked, "or is that just her career?"

Also on the Natalie bandwagon was costar Stockard Channing, who played Thelma "Sister" Husband in the film. Channing told Jensen that Natalie reminded her of actress Audrey Hepburn and possessed "that kind of simplicity, and variety, and intelligence that's genuinely there."

Praise from her professional peers is difficult for Natalie to take, primarily because she doesn't think she deserves it. That may be because she has never tackled an emotionally tough role, one that would require her to dig deep within herself. The closest she'd ever come was in *Anywhere but Here*; however, as emotional as the relationship was between Natalie and Susan Sarandon, it wasn't all that far removed from her relationship with her real-life mother.

Natalie got to the heart of the matter in an interview with Carrie Slone of *Mademoiselle*, who went to Austin to hang out with the actress during filming. Natalie told her about a game she played with Ashley called Druthers, a mind game in which the players are asked to choose one possibility over another.

Ashley asked: "Would you rather do one amazing film that goes down in history, and have a really horrible time making it, or would you rather make a lot of pretty good little films and have a great time?"

Natalie responded: "I'd rather do a lot of little ones. Maybe that's selfish; maybe it's not the artist's answer. But I'd rather behappy."

During their downtime, the two women often played games together: Trivial Pursuit, Pictionary, card games, and brainteasers. Natalie was amazed at how much Ashley knew about a wide range of subjects. She bonded with Ashley like she'd done with no other actor in her career, and they continued to share thoughts via e-mail messages long after work on the film was completed.

Natalie found working with Ashley both exhilarating and daunting at the same time. Exhilarating because she considered Ashley the best actress she had ever worked with and daunting because she sometimes felt as though she was attending acting school. "We have one long scene together and I found myself just watching her work," confessed Natalie to the *Ottawa Citizen*. "I had to keep reminding myself that I was supposed to be in the scene as well."

Another person Natalie bonded with while in Austin was the techno-pop singer Richard Hall, better known to his fans as Moby. On an evening off from filming, Natalie went to a concert to hear him perform. She was so impressed that she went backstage to introduce herself. He didn't know who she was, but he thought she was cute, so they exchanged fax numbers and e-mail addresses.

*　　*　　*

Where the Heart Is begins with Natalie and her boyfriend, Willy Jack (played by Dylan Bruno), leaving her Tennessee mobile home for the promised land of Bakersfield, California. Natalie says she hopes they find a house that overlooks the ocean, adding that she's "never lived anyplace that didn't have wheels under it."

While passing through Sequoyah, Oklahoma, a very pregnant Natalie asks Dylan to stop at a Wal-Mart so she can go to the bathroom. When she returns to the parking lot, she discovers that Dylan has abandoned her, leaving behind her only possession, a camera. Still hopeful he will return, she waits for him outside the store. It is at this point that Natalie meets Stockard Channing's character. Since Stockard works as the town's official greeter, she presents Natalie with a small bag of gifts and coupons and a small Buckeye tree potted in an old paint can.

When it becomes obvious that Dylan will not return, Natalie sets up house in the Wal-Mart, surreptitiously living in the store while she figures out what to do next. Her appearance was changed somewhat for this role. Her hair color was lightened, and blonde extensions were added to her hair to make it longer. Beneath her dress, she wore a prosthetic device that made her look pregnant. And inside her bra, she wore padding to make her breasts look larger.

Natalie didn't mind the hair extensions, and she thought the prosthetic device was sort of exciting. Before leaving for Texas (this was the first film she made without at least one of her parents being present), she wore the device around the house to get used to it, presenting an image that made her mother take big gulps of reality. Natalie also wore the device in Texas, going into a Wal-Mart store when they weren't filming so that she could get the reactions of customers who did not recognize her as a movie star.

Ashley's character is pregnant at one point in the film, so Ashley also wore a stomach prosthetic. Since the extra padding was uncomfortable in the Texas heat, the ever-resourceful Ashley showed Natalie how to put an icepack beneath her clothing between the prosthetic and her stomach.

The only thing that made Natalie laugh—and perhaps harbor hurt feelings at the same time—was the padding she had to wear in her bra. She understood that she needed it because pregnant women have enlarged breasts, but it still fostered images of teen rival Britney Spears, and they sometimes hit a little too close to home. Typically, though, Natalie dealt with the bra padding with good humor. While being interviewed by *Mademoiselle*, she gleefully reached into her bra and yanked out the fake breasts to show to the writer. "I'm not waif-thin but I'm small, so they make me wear fake boobs," she explained. "Otherwise they say I look boyish."

One day, while still living in the Wal-Mart, Natalie goes to the library to find a book that will tell her how to care for her ailing Buckeye tree. There she meets librarian Forney Hull (played by James Frain), an emotionally displaced young man who falls in love with her on the spot.

Soon after that meeting, Natalie goes into labor in the Wal-Mart. A man she later learns is Frain jumps through the store window to deliver the baby. The next morning, she awakens in the hospital, where she meets for the first time Ashley's character, a nurse named Lexie Coop.

"Am I in trouble?" Natalie asks. "Are they going to arrest me?"

"What for?" says Ashley.

"For living in the Wal-Mart?"

As it turns out, Natalie has nothing to worry about. The incident makes her a media celebrity, and not only does Wal-Mart not prosecute her, but it also gives her five hundred dollars to help her pay bills and then offers her a job working in the store.

One of the best scenes in the movie occurs after Ashley's character has been beaten by a child molester she's allowed into her home as a suitor. This is the scene that Natalie referred to earlier when talking about Ashley's acting skills. Ashley tells Natalie what happened the night she was beaten.

"How did he find me, Novalee?" asks Ashley. "How do men like that find my kids? How did he know he could do such a thing as that to us?"

Natalie comforts her by telling her that "our lives can change with every breath we take. . . . [Y]ou tell them [your kids] that we've all got meanness in us, but we got goodness, too, and the only thing worth living for is the good."

In time, Natalie develops a romantic relationship with Frain. She has mixed feelings about it but goes to bed with him after he is devastated by the death of his sister. It was her first love scene in a movie, and, while it is Disney-like in its intensity, it was difficult for her to do.

"It was probably like my worst day on the set," Natalie told *Entertainment Weekly*. "I had a really hard time. . . . I felt really weird having to kiss someone and, you know, 'fake make love' to someone, you know, I really didn't want to do that with. No offense to James, but I'm not in love with him."

The thought that a woman would kiss or make love to a man she didn't love was beyond Natalie's comprehension. Because of the protective bubble in which Natalie had lived for her entire life, she was unaware of an entire spectrum of human experience. It was the reason she'd been reluctant to do love scenes.

Other aspects of her character's life Natalie thought she could easily relate to and appreciate. "Her main problem is just believing in herself and believing that other people can like her," she told the *Ottawa Citizen*. "As an actor that's always in the back of your mind as well: Is this or that person really fond of me or do they want to use me? That's a kind of sad, sad thing to think about. . . . For Novalee, she keeps wondering whether, for example, people really like her or are just using her for sex so she has this lack of confidence in relationships."

Chapter 7

Harvard Beckons: Free at Last

Over the years, Harvard University has had its share of celebrity sightings, whether of students or of visiting dignitaries, but nothing has ever rattled the campus quite as much as the arrival of Natalie Hershlag.

Yes, for educational purposes, she left Natalie Portman at the door.

Frankly, the buzz around Natalie probably had less to do with her as an experienced actress—few students associated her with *The Professional*, *Beautiful Girls*, or *Anywhere but Here*—as it did with her role in *Star Wars: The Phantom Menace*.

Natalie was just a student, while Queen Amidala was, well, the prominent and mysterious ruler of the planet Naboo. Added to that was the realization that Natalie and Queen Amidala were probably the most famous virgins in the universe. For the average student, male or female, that virginity offered a challenge of intriguing possibilities. It was the stuff of which early-morning dreams are made.

Of course, not everyone was out to nail Natalie her first week of school. Most encounters with her were fortuitous. Brandon Renken, an eighteen-year-old freshman from Houston, bumped into her during the first few days of class. "It was kind of weird because I had just walked over to see what plans one of my roommates had for the rest of the day, and he happened to be talking to a group of girls, of which Natalie happened to be one," he recalled. "When she introduced herself, she did so kind of timidly, just like any other girl would on the first few days of classes, meeting so many new people and not being entirely certain how to keep track of them all."

When Natalie extended her hand and said "I'm Natalie," all Renken could think about was that he'd camped out at a movie theater in Houston to purchase tickets for *The Phantom Menace*. "That was really the only awkward part, feeling like I already knew a little bit about her even though I had never actually met her before," he said. "I guess it's that way with all celebrities. They are all over the news and movies, so you feel like you have some knowledge of who they are."

Another student who literally bumped into Natalie was Jeff Kazen. They were in the same lunch line when a sudden surge of hungry students knocked them together. "At first, I just thought it was another student," he recalled. "When I noticed it was her, I was a little bit more embarrassed than if I had bumped into any average student. We both said sorry, and that was all. I must say when I first saw her (which was much earlier than this time) she was a lot shorter than I expected but definitely as pretty as I had pictured her."

While students may have been concerned about meeting Natalie, or not meeting her, she had much greater concerns. Her list of things to do at Harvard went far beyond reminders to "do the laundry" or "go to the library." Natalie was concerned that her roommates (she had three) would be influenced by her stardom. Would they hate her because of it? Or would they pretend to like her when they really did not? She was worried about both overachieving and underachieving. She was concerned about how her professors would react to her. Would they be jealous of her stardom and seek to make an example out of her in the classroom? Or would they embarrass her with unearned compliments about her work?

Before Natalie left for college, one of her friends called and asked who her roommates would be. Natalie said she didn't know. Her friend voiced concern that her roommates might be intimidated by bunking with a movie star. Natalie had never thought about it exactly that way. It was she who felt intimidated. Nonetheless, her friend's comments upset her because more than anything else she wanted a normal relationship with normal roommates.

Natalie was assigned to Lowell House, one of twelve undergraduate houses at Harvard. Constructed in 1930, it was named for the Lowell family, which had been associated with the university since John Lowell graduated in 1721. The house accommodates over five hundred people, about 450 of whom are undergraduate students.

There are no *Star Wars* posters in the dining hall, but there are portraits of Abbott Lawrence Lowell, president of the university from 1909 to 1933, and his brother, Percival, an astronomer who discovered the planet Pluto. There is also a portrait of their sister, Amy, a headstrong woman best known perhaps for introducing author D.H. Lawrence to American readers and for linking the Lowell name to a scandal or two. No matter where Natalie sat in the dining hall, Amy's piercing eyes seemed to follow her.

Natalie's worst fears about her roommates were never realized. They turned out to be young women much like Natalie, having enrolled at Harvard to get an education. If they were impressed to be rooming with a movie star, they never allowed their enthusiasm to proceed past polite compliments on her work.

If anyone at Harvard was truly impressed by her peers, it was Natalie. "All my classmates have accomplishments—in Olympic athletics, music, poetry, lots of talents," she told the Nashville *Tennessean*. "The only thing that makes me different is that I happen to work in an area which gets lots

134

of media attention. There is one little problem. I'm short and have dark hair. A lot of people look like me. People who have heard I'm on campus are always spotting me at places where I'm not."

It is the sort of thing that keeps Natalie on her toes. Soon after starting classes, she received a call from her dean. Word was out that she had been spotted at a local bar. The dean wanted to know if it was true and why she was hanging out in a bar. Natalie was horrified. Not so much because of a rumor floating about that she was sneaking into bars, but because of the suggestion that she would do so to have a few drinks. She is a teetotaler, and the very thought of downing a couple of beers is as repulsive to her vegetarian code of ethics as is the thought of eating a thick, charcoal-grilled beefsteak with a side order of veal.

Natalie wasn't the only student suffering from mistaken identity. Once word got out that she was at Harvard, some of her hard-core fans made an effort to locate her. The first thing they learned was that no Natalie Portman was enrolled at the university. She had entered the school under another name. Since Harvard, like most other universities, has a student directory that lists the e-mail addresses and telephone numbers of registered students, Natalie's fans launched an assault against *all* Natalies listed in the directory. The fans called and sent e-mails to every Natalie on campus. The *Harvard Crimson* wrote a story about the havoc under the headline "Natalie's Here, There, and Everywhere." Unfortunately for the fans, Natalie isn't listed in the student directory and doesn't use a university e-mail address.

For Natalie Lester, class of 2001, it was a nightmare. "One time there was this little boy really obsessed with *Star Wars*, not [with] her, and he added me to his *Star Wars* fan club email list," she told the *Crimson*. "[He]

135

kept sending me all his info on the movies until I begged him to take me off his list."

All that misdirected loyalty embarrassed the real Natalie, the same way her parents embarrassed her when they danced together or showed affection for each other in public, but there was nothing she could do about it, so she simply ignored it and hoped everyone else would ignore it as well.

Academically, Natalie seemed to blend in quite well. In media interviews, whenever she heaped praise on the accomplishments of other students, which she often did, she had in mind students such as Connie Kim, a psychology major from Iowa. In addition to her studies in psychology—her senior honors thesis will be on the "Frog Pond Effect" at Harvard—Kim was the producer of the Harvard production of Eve Ensler's controversial play *Vagina Monologues*.

Kim and Natalie were classmates in a science course designed to teach students about the human brain. "I was quite impressed by the level and extent of Natalie's understanding of the course material," said Kim. "She arrived on time for section (something that most Harvard students do not generally do) . . . and she came prepared to answer and to ask questions which showed the depth of her knowledge. In fact, she often explained difficult concepts to other students when they could not understand something the [teaching fellow] was explaining. So yes, Natalie was a terrific student, probably better than most other students."

Harvard was pretty much what Natalie had expected. She knew going in that she would have to study hard to make the grades she and her parents expected. However, what surprised her were the many unforeseen distractions that competed for her time. Parties and student events fell into that category. She did not want to ignore them, because they are so much a part of university life. And then there were things she wanted to ignore but could not—such as doing the laundry.

Before arriving on campus, Natalie had never done her own laundry. Once she settled into her dorm room, she quickly learned that if she did not do her own laundry, then it simply would not get done. She coped by stuffing her dirty clothes into oversized plastic garbage bags. Out of sight, out of mind. Of course, when the time came to do the laundry, she ended up using twice as many machines as the other students, looking every bit the self-indulgent movie star she thought she wasn't.

*   *   *

In September 1999, Natalie had been at Harvard for only one week when she did something that could best be described as very un-collegiate—she flew to Canada to participate in the Toronto International Film Festival.

While other students in her residence hall were cracking the books and washing their laundry, Natalie was hanging out with Susan Sarandon and Wayne Wang to help promote *Anywhere but Here*. Although the movie was not scheduled to be released until November, it was previewed in Toronto, where it received an enthusiastic reception.

At a press conference, Natalie was asked how she was most like and unlike Ann, the character she played in the movie. The question seemed to catch her off guard (perhaps she was thinking about her class on the workings of the human brain, or perhaps she was thinking about how the trip to Canada would only add to her laundry bag).

"Go ahead, honey," Sarandon said, laughing. "And smile when you do it."

Natalie laughed too. Sarandon has an ability to be wicked and embracing at the same instant. It is one of the qualities that women like

137

about her. After a few moments, Natalie answered the question: "I think I'm very like Ann in my desires for who I want to be and the things I want to do with my life. Education is very important to me, and going away and being independent, and . . . becoming an adult in a way that is close to my parents, but yet independent from them, is a big thing that I'm experiencing right now. . . . [But] I never really went through the problems with my parents that Ann went through with her mother."

Natalie was asked what school she attended.

"I'm not talking about that," she said.

Later during the press conference, someone again asked her what college she attended. "I'm not telling," Natalie said and laughed. "I'm not trying to—"

Sarandon, still playing the role of the protective mother, interrupted Natalie. "She's not telling," Sarandon said, chiding the media. "So don't keep asking. She's not going to tell you."

Before leaving Toronto, Natalie, wearing sandals and a diaphanous black gown, attended a cocktail party at a festival bar named Easy & The Fifth. It must have driven her crazy, all that booze and dead meat on little crackers—hopefully, someone had a celery stick there for her to munch on—but she was a trooper and went through the motions with a broad smile on her face.

Natalie may have returned to Harvard with a sense of dread. She knew she had more high-profile media interviews to do that semester, and she couldn't help but worry about how they might affect the way other students would treat her.

Natalie loved being a student, and she loved being in movies. It was inevitable that she would feel guilt whenever she put one passion ahead of the other. It is amazing when you think about it that she did not turn to drugs or alcohol to ease the stress. Many people in her position would have resorted to chemical salves, and the fact that she didn't is a reflection of the character that her parents instilled in her.

Nonetheless, the show must go on.

In November, Natalie met Sarandon again for a joint appearance on the *Oprah Winfrey Show*. Oprah asked Natalie if she was having a good time in college, though she didn't even bother to ask her which college, and Natalie responded by gently correcting her.

"Working hard," she said.

"*Anywhere but Here*—was it sort of reminiscent of anything you had to go through when you had to leave home with your own mom?" Oprah asked.

"I have a much more, I guess, what we would call normal relationship with my mother in that she's very mature and responsible," answered Natalie.

Oprah said she thought the movie mom is "wacked."

"I think that that move from being dependent [on] and protected by your parents to being all of a sudden on your own, doing your own laundry and fending for yourself, it's a big move. And, also, I'm an only child, so it was a huge deal."

Natalie went on to say that her mother had replaced her with animals. Since they already had a dog, Noodles, she said her mother had gone shopping for a rabbit. When she'd found one she liked, she'd taken Noodles into the pet store to get its reaction.

"Not normal at all," commented Natalie with a smile.

On November 11, 1999, Natalie returned to *The Late Show with David Letterman*. He complimented her on how beautiful she looked, which he always does when she is on the show, only this time he observed that "now you're all grown up, for heaven's sake." That was the sort of comment that endeared him to Natalie.

She was there to promote *Anywhere but Here*, but as usual Letterman held off on mentioning the film until near the end of the interview. That is one thing that is predictable about her appearances on the show. She and Letterman seem to enter into an unspoken conspiracy to have fun and to talk about her movie projects as little as possible. It is their little secret. If he were about thirty years younger, he would be the perfect soul mate for Natalie. At some level, she seems to understand that.

More than the movie, which some critics uncharitably called a chick flick, Letterman was interested in her college adventures.

"How's that going?" he asked.

"It's good . . . [but] it's hard."

He asked Natalie how she thought she'd fare when the grades were issued.

"I'm a little nervous, but I think it'll be OK."

When Letterman inquired about the courses she was taking, she told him about her chemistry class. That piqued his interest, and he asked what things they did in the classroom.

"You know, basic chemistry things," she explained. "We blow things up and—"

Letterman interrupted her with his "perplexed man" look, sending the audience into hysterical laughter.

Natalie good-naturedly continued, "My professors are going to, like, kill me when I get back."

If Natalie thought her "blowing things up" imagery was titillating, it was nothing compared to what lay in store once Letterman started questioning her about her social life at college. She proceeded to tell him about a party called the "Debauchery Ball."

Hosted each year by Winthrop House, one of Harvard's upper-class dormitories, the Debauchery Ball invites students to attend wearing a minimum of clothing. Once there, they are sold "debauchery money" (fake money they can purchase for about five dollars) that they can use to bribe other students to engage in scandalous acts. At the end of the evening, the individual or team with the most fake money is declared the winner.

Other dormitories have similar parties—Kirkland House calls its party "Incest Fest" and allows only residents to attend, and Pforzheimer House calls its party "PfoHo 54" and jazzes things up with neon lights, spinning balls, and glittered faces.

Of course, the Debauchery Ball isn't as bad as its name suggests—basically, it is just a dance party with a hot band—but students do try to push the envelope in order to conform to the party's decadent theme.

Natalie did not explain all the details to Letterman, but she did disclose that the theme involved offering fake money to other students in exchange for favors.

"It was a little scary at first," she said, "but my friend Vicki and I went, and we just kind of hung back and were voyeurs instead of participants."

Pressed about whether students had got "fresh" with her at the party, Natalie probably went a little further than she intended by saying, "I had a girl come up to me and [say] like, 'Can I kiss you for one hundred dollars—and I was like, 'No!'"

Letterman's reaction was predictable. He reached for pen and paper, as if to take down the girl's name, and he jokingly offered to give Natalie his business card to take back to the girl with the hundred dollars. Everyone had a good laugh, including Natalie, but she must have cringed a little for ratting on Winthrop House.

When she returned to campus, she was greeted a few days later with a mention in the weekly *Harvard Independent*. Under the headline "Thanks Natalie!" the newspaper recounted the Letterman experience, including his comment about the girl who wanted to trade a hundred dollars for a smooch with Natalie. The girl who offered the money has a most distinctive first name, so it will not be divulged here, but suffice it to say that, when she was approached about giving her side of the story, she froze in her tracks like a deer caught in the proverbial headlights. Too bad! There was a hundred bucks in it for her—with or without a smooch!

* * *

Nothing Natalie had done or seen in life had prepared her for Harvard. True, she'd had life experiences that most of her classmates would never have, but for the most part those experiences had occurred under a protective bubble. She was wise beyond her years, though not necessarily in matters important to her classmates.

The Debauchery Ball was a real eye-opener for Natalie.

Most of her female classmates and dorm mates were concerned more about what kind of birth control to use than about whether they should have sex. They talked about what kind of sex was appropriate on a first date. They talked about orgasms, oral sex, and missed periods. Natalie never excused herself from those conversations, but, unlike most other subjects, she never had much to contribute, unless it was something one of her costars had told her. Those conversations made her feel inadequate among her peers, and it wasn't a feeling she enjoyed having.

Each April for the past sixteen years, the *Harvard Independent* has conducted a student survey, two portions of which deal with sex and drug use. Every year Natalie has been at Harvard, the dormitory with the most libidinous population has been . . . you guessed it, Winthrop House, the home of the Debauchery Ball.

In 2001, 53.8 percent of the respondents from Winthrop admitted to having had sex during the preceding month. Not far behind was Natalie's dorm, where about half the residents who filled out questionnaires said they had done the Big Dirty within the past month. The overall average was better for freshman as a whole, indicating that 58 percent had never had sex. "Don't worry," said the *Independent*. "The virgin percentage drops to 28 percent by senior year."

Not surprisingly, sex was the number-one topic of conversation on campus. It prompted one student, Rebecca L. Torres, to write a column for the *Independent* in which she bemoaned the results of the sex survey and the fact that, for her at least, the "dating scene at Harvard sucks." What she wanted to know was "Who are these students that are satisfied with their dating life and how can I meet them?"

All of this had a major impact on Natalie. Not only were her hormones flowing like gasoline on ninety-nine-cents-a-gallon day, but also she was dealing with the Britney Spears syndrome. Unlike other students, she had to make decisions about both her sex life and her film career as an adult woman.

Natalie cracked jokes during the filming of *Where the Heart Is* about wearing pads in her bra, but how easy is it for any eighteen-year-old woman to hear that her chest is so flat it makes her look "boyish?" Jokes aside, it had to be painful for her, all the more so when she got to Harvard and was surrounded by thousands of better endowed female students, many of whom were equally as beautiful and accomplished.

When Natalie was still in high school, she had a friend who had cosmetic surgery on her nose. Natalie thought that was fine, she had no major issues with it, but she liked the way her friend looked before the surgery. To be competitive as an actress, would Natalie have to undergo breast augmentation? Exactly how much demand was there for actresses with "boyish" figures?

By the end of her first term at Harvard, Natalie was in shell shock. Nothing she had experienced making films or attending Syosset High School had prepared her for Harvard. "You're faced with . . . [making wrong choices] every day," she told the *Los Angeles Daily News*. "You're deciding how you want to define yourself in a new situation. You don't know anybody, and you're trying to present an image of yourself to people. And you have to figure out who you are in order to do that, and that's hard and confusing."

During winter recess, Natalie felt like she needed a break, so she went with friends to the Caribbean for a few days of rest and relaxation. It was only the second time she had gone away without her parents (the first being her trip to Texas), and she felt like a grownup woman, perhaps for the first time in her life.

With her hair pulled back, Natalie hit the beach with her friends, where they soaked up the sun like collegiate sponges. In no time at all, she was sunburned from head to foot. On the second or third day, wearing a paisley-like bikini, she stretched out on a blue beach towel and underwent an epiphany of the sort young women experience from time to time. Without a word of explanation to her friends, she whipped off her bikini top and lay on her back. The moment was captured on film by a photographer who sold the photos to a British tabloid. Within days, the photos were plastered all over the Internet. The actress who had sworn she would never do a nude scene was now topless on a public beach. Why would Natalie do such a thing, especially in a public place?

Not surprisingly, her publicist declined to comment. But there may have been two reasons. First, Natalie may just have wanted to do something bold to prove to herself that she had it in her to be rebellious. There is a good reason why parents cringe when their children leave home for the first time: all too often they feel compelled to experiment with the very things their parents have warned them about since the onset of puberty. It has been a rite of passage since the arrival of upright walking. Since Natalie did not do drugs or alcohol—and wasn't yet ready to have sex—she had few alternatives left.

Second, Natalie may have wanted to prove that she doesn't look "boyish." Natalie may have noticed the photographers roaming about on the beach and decided to prove to the world, herself most of all, that she doesn't have a boyish figure.

*   *   *

Within days of her return to classes, Natalie was subjected to yet another reminder that she was more than just another student. On January 23, 2000, the Hollywood Foreign Press Association held its annual Golden Globe Awards.

For her work in *Anywhere but Here*, Natalie had been nominated for Best Performance by an Actress in a Supporting Role, her first nomination for an acting award. Also nominated were Cameron Diaz for *Being John Malkovich*, Angelina Jolie for *Girl, Interrupted*, Catherine Keener for *Being John Malkovich*, and Chloe Sevigny for *Boys Don't Cry*. When the award was announced, it was Jolie who went to the stage, not Natalie, but that was all right because Jolie had indeed delivered a memorable performance, and all the movies named in that category are extraordinary,

145

and there is no shame in losing to actresses and films of that caliber. Although Natalie didn't win, later that year she did take home a YoungStar Award for Best Young Actress/Performance in a Motion Picture Comedy.

There was no uproar on campus about Natalie's topless romp, and why would there have been? Only a dork would criticize her for that. What Harvard coed hadn't ditched her bra in public at some point in her life? Certainly, Amy Lowell would have understood. The photos did nothing to dampen Natalie's social agenda, for she made certain that she balanced her studying with a decent amount of playtime. Sometimes the playtime got her into trouble, such as the time she and her friends went to a Moby concert, only to be turned away at the door. According to newspaper articles, she was turned away for using a fake ID. Not so, protested Natalie, who explained that Moby was a good friend of hers and had put her on his guest list for the concert. When she and her friends arrived, they were told the guest list had been closed. Natalie was embarrassed by the incident, so she and her friends left the venue and went home, end of story.

One of the extracurricular organizations Natalie got involved in was a coed social group named the Hasty Pudding. Members are chosen by a process called "punching." The would-be member presents himself or herself to the entire membership in a social situation that allows for mingling. It is similar to "rush," the process by which "pledges" are evaluated by Greek fraternities and sororities. Natalie attended the initial Hasty Pudding punching, then returned for a few more events, during which everyone was given a good going over. She made it all the way to the final dinner, after which she was asked to perform a skit in front of the guests. The Hasty Puddings then extended to Natalie an invitation to join, and she accepted.

The Hasty Pudding was not the only social organization Natalie visited. During her final year of high school, she'd visited the Harvard campus and attended a party held by the Owls. Called the Lu'au, it has a reputation among students as the most anticipated social event of the year. Earlier that year, it had been written up in a national magazine as being one of the best college parties in the nation.

The third party Natalie attended was sponsored by Phoenix, an all-male "finals" club that typically sponsors a formal "punch" event each year. If members and guests are not currently dating, they will typically show up at the party with the best-looking women they can cajole into accompanying them.

Somehow Natalie ended up on the arm of a Phoenix guest. What better way to impress the membership than by showing up with a movie star on your arm? Natalie had a splendid time at the party, reveling in the spotlight—observers said she "danced like a maniac"—but it is doubtful she would have had such a good time if she'd known about the chickens. If you recall, Natalie gave up eating meat at an early age after seeing a chicken killed as part of an experiment at a medical convention.

In 1999, members of Phoenix attracted a lot of attention when club elders decided to require newly elected members to carry a live chicken with them when they made their appointed rounds to classes and social events. Since not all the new members had farm experience, most elected to carry their chickens in boxes about one foot square.

Not everyone on campus was happy about the chickens. Particularly upset was Marc D. Hauser, a professor of psychology in the Mind, Brain, and Behavior Program. In an article published in the *Harvard Crimson*, he said it was a "deeply worrying situation," adding that, "like humans, chickens have emotions and thoughts." Professor Hauser said the chicken affair was inexcusable. "It should never have started and should stop immediately. One hopes that these students will feel remorse concerning their pathetic treatment of a creature that shares this planet with us."

Just when men began to make sense to her, Natalie was subjected to the sight of male students scurrying across campus with terrified chickens under their arms. Was it any wonder that she was in no hurry to attach herself to a Harvard man? Besides, what man dumb enough to carry a chicken around the campus would be smart enough to maintain a relationship with Natalie?

Interviewed around that time by *E! Online* about the stresses of "coming of age," Natalie said that learning to take care of herself hadn't been easy. "You realize everyone isn't good and people will disappoint you," she said, perhaps thinking about the chickens. "There are moments when I think everyone is evil! But you get beyond that." Asked if the "evil" ones were male, she laughed and answered, "I'm not saying—if you don't have anything nice to say. . . ."

* * *

By the end of her first term at Harvard, Natalie had acquired an entourage, which for the sake of convenience we will call "Nat's Nadirs." Wherever she goes on campus, her stealthy admirers follow her. Sometimes they simply appear in classrooms or at social functions, as if they have parachuted in on assignment.

As you might have guessed, Nat's Nadirs is almost exclusively a boys' club. The boys don't wear T-shirts with Nat's Nadirs printed on them or wear lapel pins with Queen Amidala's image on them, but in their energetic earnestness they do stand out in a crowd, much as Secret Service agents stand out whenever the president is in the vicinity.

148

Brandon Molina, a biology major from Tampa, had never seen *Star Wars*, and he knew nothing about Natalie Portman, except that she was a celebrity student people talked about . . . and she was in one of his classes.

One day Molina walked into class with two friends who knew everything there was to know about Natalie and her film career. "They were on the lookout for her and had noticed where she usually sat so we could get as close as possible," Molina recalled. "Class went on, and no one made much mention of her. At the end, everyone was standing [around] waiting to file out of the class. In my booming voice, I said, 'See, all of that preparation and you still didn't catch that Queen Ama-dama-ding-dong girl you were looking for. I guess the Force wasn't with you.'"

With that, Nat's Nadirs, working in unison, snapped their heads around and emitted a stream of dirty looks in Molina's direction. It is a look that anyone writing a book about Natalie would instantly recognize, even if it were offered only via e-mail. One zealous member of Nat's Nadirs fired off an e-mail that referred to the "inadvisability and inappropriateness" of a biography of the movie star.

Better watch out, buster, the e-mail suggested, *we got chickens!*

In the spring of 2001, it was a subject that led to spirited debate on campus, the general theme of which was "Someone is writing a book about one of our own, so what are we going to do about it?" Soman Chainani, a staff writer at the *Harvard Crimson*, joined in that debate by reprinting the author's queries to various students in the newspaper.

Although Chainani's articles were most helpful in the general pursuit of knowledge, some of his comments indicated that Chainani had a conflict between loyalty to Natalie, who just happened to be one of his dorm mates, and loyalty to the higher purposes of journalism to which he aspired. He ultimately came down on the side of good journalism, but the journey took a tortuous route.

During Natalie's first year at Harvard, the university was home to two well-known actors—Jonathan Taylor Thomas, of *Home Improvement* fame, and Elisabeth Shue, a gifted actress who is probably best known for her role as a prostitute in *Leaving Las Vegas* (1995)—yet neither one was subjected to anything close to the adulation of Nat's Nadirs. That may have been because Shue was considered damaged goods as a result of her stint as a cinematic hooker and because Thomas was the wrong sex to inspire a public display of unbridled adulation, but, whatever the reason, it is a certainty that it was not instigated by Natalie.

What Natalie wanted more than anything else from her classmates was simply to be treated as just another student. Most Harvard students were happy to oblige. Many view on-campus celebrities as a fact of life. "I rather enjoy having celebrities attend Harvard," said Jeff Kazen. "It's something to brag about to friends, and, although they have special privacy policies for them, it hasn't done anything to affect my experience at Harvard. I feel that the additional privacy is necessary. . . . [W]ithout it, I feel that going to any college would be difficult for a celebrity."

Harvard officials were asked to explain their special policies toward celebrity students but declined to do so, perhaps for fear of appearing to be starstruck or ungrateful for celebrity endowments.

"I don't really know if there are special rules for celebrity students," observed Brandon Renken, "but if there are they must be effective, because there is no media or student spectacle surrounding any of the celebrities I have encountered on campus, and it's not like they hide out in their dorm rooms—we leave that for computer science majors. I really don't think that television and movie stars are of the biggest concern for Harvard. There are sons and daughters of important political figures that I am sure pose more difficulties and children of millionaires that also seem like they would be more problematic for the university to keep safe and unexploited than Natalie Portman or Jonathan Taylor Thomas. In the end, we all have to take midterms and cope with the core. We're all moderately intelligent students paying more than most of us can afford in the hopes that our future will be as promising as that of Harvard graduates before us."

One thing that has endeared Natalie to other students was her determination to soak up the Harvard experience, regardless of the celebrity baggage that always threatened to hold her back. In addition to joining the Hasty Pudding club, Natalie participated in a community service volunteer program called CityStep. Actually, it is a joint venture between Harvard and Radcliffe College, the purpose of which is to expose Cambridge elementary school students to the arts through a curriculum of improvised and choreographed skits and programs. An important goal of the organization is to overcome racism and socioeconomic polarization by mixing a demographically diverse grammar school population with idealistic Harvard and Radcliffe students who are as open to receiving new experiences as they are to offering new experiences to the children with whom they work.

The CityStep program operates from October until the following April and ends with a show designed and choreographed by the Harvard-Radcliffe students and their pupils. Shortly after the project begins, usually in November, the Harvard-Radcliffe students hold a benefit ball to raise money for CityStep. The event is so popular that it usually sells out, making tickets difficult to come by.

"The year that Natalie was involved in the program was no exception," said Connie Kim. "I actually did attend the ball that year and, in the midst

151

of my dancing and mingling with other students, happened to see Natalie waltz in with a dark-colored dress (I believe it was black), incredibly high heels, and her beau on her arm. Her boyfriend at that time was a junior, a star on Harvard's swim team, and very, very tall and quite blond. It was probably a good thing that Natalie was wearing heels, thinking back, because it probably would have been hard for the two to dance together otherwise, due to the difference in height."

*   *   *

Where the Heart Is was released on April 28, 2000 to theaters across the country. Critics were not kind. Writing in the *Chicago Sun-Times*, Roger Ebert praised Natalie and Ashley for their acting skills but said that the film is one in which "melodramatic elements are slapped on top of one another like a hurry-up plaster-boarding job." San Francisco *Examiner* critic Wesley Morris said that Natalie's relationship with Frain "seems more like a public service than real passion, rendering her a polite cipher that not even Portman's blinding, burgeoning stardom can make real."

Todd Camp of the Fort Worth *Star-Telegram* gagged over yet another cinematic reference to Southern trailer parks and discount stores, but he saw merit in the performances: "Though her uneducated, hopelessly naïve Novalee sometimes comes across as a glamour queen whose shine has been dulled just a bit by greasy hair and makeup shadows under her eyes, Portman exudes so much charm it's hard not to root for her."

Some days Natalie must have wondered why she even bothered to get out of bed.

*   *   *

As Natalie prepared to celebrate her nineteenth birthday in June 2000, tragedy struck, reminding her not only of her own mortality but also of the fleeting, sometimes fragile, nature of family bonds. Her Israeli

152

grandmother, her father's mother, passed away. For the first time, Natalie understood that becoming an adult involves so much more than coming and going as one pleases; it also involves the loss of loved ones, the acceptance of emotional pain, and loneliness as the price one pays for having life.

Natalie traveled to Israel with her parents to attend the funeral or shivah, as it is called in Jewish tradition. It was a journey she'd made two or three times a year for the past decade, but never before with such a heavy heart. Of all her relatives, it was her grandmother Hershlag who'd doted on her the most. The only member of Natalie's family to ever give a television interview, she'd proudly displayed photographs of her granddaughter on the walls of her apartment.

Sadness had never been a big part of Natalie's life. Now Natalie would have to learn to live with it, just as she had learned to live with being born a Jew in Jerusalem, ground zero of the apocalyptic second coming of the Messiah.

By her own admission, Natalie is not an observant Jew. To the extent that she thinks of herself as a Jew, she does so as an Israeli Jew, which means that she puts the ethnic and cultural values of Judaism ahead of religious considerations. She has told reporters that she is not very religious and does not believe in an afterlife.

The trip to Israel placed a heavy burden on Natalie for another reason. A few weeks before her grandmother died, Natalie did an interview with the *Yediot Achronoth*, Israel's largest daily newspaper. According to the reporter who interviewed her, she said she had received a draft notice from the Israeli army but had "passed" on it because it would have postponed her studies until she was twenty-one.

153

Reaction to the story was almost immediate. Newspaper stories around the world declared Natalie a "draft dodger" who had refused to serve her country. Male Israelis are required to serve three years in the army, and female Israelis are required to serve twenty-one months. Shouldn't Natalie, of proud Hershlag lineage after all, be required to live up to the promise of her Zionist ancestors?

Her publicist denied that the Israeli newspaper had ever interviewed Natalie. "She was never notified by the army for service," explained the publicist, because she is "exempt from the army." Contacted by reporters, an official at the Israeli consulate in New York backed up the publicist's story, affirming that if Natalie had left Israel before the age of sixteen and was not currently living there, she was exempt from military service.

Only later did Natalie herself clarify the issue. "This is really a silly story about my own stupidity," she told *People* magazine. "I said in passing, in an interview, 'Yeah, I dodged the draft,' and then they [the media] made this big deal out of it. . . . [I]t was my own stupid mistake, and I stand corrected."

All that must have been on her mind as she attended her grandmother's funeral. Not only had Natalie lost someone who'd been very dear to her, but also she had to wonder if her grandmother had read the story about the draft—and if she had believed it.

Then there was the matter of her identity as an Israeli and a Jew. The older Natalie became, the more complex her life seemed to be, especially as it related to what others expected of her. She was proud of having been born in Israel, but she was now an American. Would there ever come a time when she could simply be Natalie?

After completing the shivah, a seven-day gathering at the home of the deceased, Natalie was driven to the Tel-Aviv airport. Waiting for her

154

departure flight was sheer agony for her, especially after being so immersed in the mourning process. Just as she had flown off as a child, away from her grandmother's loving arms, so too was she now leaving again, only this time to make a motion picture.

As she sat in the airport, Natalie sensed that people were staring and pointing at her. A mother with a child approached her and asked if she could take a photo of Natalie with the child. Natalie said no, sending the mother and child away in a huff.

Finally, feeling alone and powerless, Natalie broke down and wept.

*　*　*

Natalie wrapped up her first year at Harvard with mixed feelings. On the plus side, she had proved to herself that she was Harvard material. She had proved to her parents that she could make it on her own. And she had proved to the movie industry that she could pursue an education while fulfilling her obligations to the production companies that invested heavily in her as an actress.

On the negative side, she had lost her grandmother, an event that struck not only at her sense of family but also at her sense of identity as an Israeli-born Jew. These were tough issues for Natalie to resolve because they had formed the core of her upbringing. Like every other student on campus, she had to determine where the expectations of her family left off and her own expectations began.

For the first eighteen years of her life, the focus had been on family and her Jewish ancestry. Everyone who had dealt with Natalie, whether in the movies or in school, had deferred to those two influences. Now she was in a student population that had no interest whatsoever in her family or in her cultural or religious background. Reactions from other students were colored, to some extent, by her celebrity, but for the most part the

155

battleground was over her thoughts on a variety of issues important to her peers. For Natalie, the question boiled down to whether she wanted to be Natalie Portman or Natalie Hershlag.

After final exams, Natalie had only a couple of weeks off before flying to Sydney, Australia, to commence work on *Star Wars: Episode II—Attack of the Clones*. Filming was set to begin on June 26, 2000. It was only the third time she'd left the United States without her parents. She did take several of her girlfriends with her, with the approval of director George Lucas, who economically used them as extras in the film.

A few weeks before school was out, Natalie appeared on *The Charlie Rose Show*. The host usually interviews authors but occasionally ventures into the glitzy worlds of television and movies. He introduced Natalie by referring to her "acclaimed body of work." He then showed a trailer for her most recent film, *Where the Heart Is*.

Although Natalie spent much of the interview talking about the film and her background as an actress, the conversation eventually made its way around to her upcoming *Star Wars* project. The first thing that impressed her about Lucas was his vision of what the *Star Wars* trilogy would be like.

"He brought me to his office, when he first was asking me to do the film, and he described to me what the film was going to look like," she said. "When someone has that vision and then completes that, I just think that is amazing. I mean, directing is so difficult, and that's why it is so hard for me to see my directors, you know, get trashed or whatever, because it is one of the hardest jobs ever, I think."

Natalie was loyal to Lucas despite the criticism he'd taken for the previous *Star Wars* film, and he repaid that loyalty in countless ways, most notably in the manner in which he chose her love interest for *Episode II—Attack of the Clones*. Since Natalie was the only actor Lucas had signed to do all three episodes, it was important to him that the actor he chose to play Anakin Skywalker display chemistry with his female lead. So Lucas invited four actors to read with Natalie. It was a high compliment to her, a consideration not many actresses receive from their directors. Lucas was realistic. Natalie was not the franchise—it was the technological wizardry of the show that would make or break it at the box office—but she was the undisputed soul of the *Star Wars* saga, the strongest "human" component, and he wanted to make certain that she cinematically bonded with the male lead.

Once the readings were finished, Lucas offered the job to nineteen-year-old Canadian actor Hayden Christensen. Lucas never announced the other candidates, but the media tossed around the names of Leonardo DiCaprio and Jonathan Jackson. Born in Vancouver, British Columbia, Christensen had been acting since the age of thirteen, but most of his work had been in made-for-television movies such as *Love and Betrayal: The Mia Farrow Story* (1995).

The entertainment industry was stunned by Lucas's decision. Christensen had a solid career as a television actor, but he had appeared in only two movies, *Street Law* and *The Virgin Suicides*. What everyone wanted to know was why Lucas would hire an unknown for such a blockbuster role. Lucas never fully explained his choice, but he didn't have to do so to insiders.

Natalie is a wonderfully expressive actress who can transform the emotions of her characters in the blink of an eye. She can break your heart without saying a word. Her only weakness as an actress is an inability to fake romantic interest in another character. She simply cannot do it, at least not at this stage of her career. Lucas had been around Natalie enough during the filming of the first episode to notice that her eyes danced and

157

sparkled when she was excited about something. The "readings" were thus meant to test her reactions to the male actors more than their reactions to her.

At six-foot-one, Christensen was the actor with the closest physical resemblance to boys Natalie had found attractive in high school and during her first year at Harvard (remember her escort to the CityStep ball?). When Lucas watched the two actors read together, he thought he saw the signs of a romantic chemistry, and he went with his gut feeling. That may seem like an inappropriate way to choose an actor for a multimillion-dollar epic, but Lucas knew that the only thing in the movie he couldn't digitalize was the chemistry between Queen Amidala and Anakin Skywalker.

If the trilogy worked the way Lucas wanted it to work, the love affair between the two characters would become one of the most celebrated in movie history. The two actors had to be convincing as lovers to audiences, and the only way Lucas could know for certain was to become an audience member during the readings. He figured he would know it when he saw it. When Christensen read with Natalie, her eyes danced. That was all Lucas needed to know. Christensen was his man.

Returning for *Episode II—Attack of the Clones* were Ewan McGregor, who played Obi-Wan Kenobi; Ian McDiarmid, who played Supreme Chancellor Palpatine and Darth Sidious; Pernilla August, who played Shmi Skywalker; and Samuel Jackson, who played Mace Windu. Joining them were a number of veteran actors, including Jimmy Smits and Christopher Lee, sporting intriguing character names such as Bail Organa, Count Dooku, and Elian Sleazebaggano.

During production, Lucas kept a tight lid on the plot for *Episode II*, but word leaked out that the key event—Anakin Skywalker's crossover to the dark side to become Darth Vader—is the result of his relationship with

Queen Amidala. Knowing what we know about the workings of Natalie's mind, she must have found it delightfully ironic that her first on-screen romance to actually be consummated sends her partner over the edge of human reason and compassion. How cool is that for a beginner?

Apparently, Lucas is an excellent judge of dancing eyes because during the nine weeks that the crew was in Australia Natalie and Hayden were often seen together away from the set, leading Australian newspaper reporters to speculate on a real-life romance. Both actors denied it, of course.

One thing that set *Episode II—Attack of the Clones* apart was Lucas's decision to make the entire movie "film free." An advocate of digital production techniques, Lucas used nothing but digital cameras to shoot the movie. The effect on the cast was minimal, most noticeable between takes because with a digital camera there is no pausing to stop and reload the camera. As a result, the actors could maintain the energy that they'd built up to carry the performance. The advantage to Lucas was that he could see dailies while they were being shot.

The disadvantage to using digital cameras was that in 2000, when the second episode was shot, there were only about forty digital projectors in use. "We're hoping by 2002 there'll be at least a couple hundred, and a couple thousand by the time the third film is out," Lucas told *Entertainment Weekly*. "But there's no way that we're going to threaten the movie theaters. That would be suicidal."

Another thing that will make *Episode II* different is its "culturally diverse" cast of characters, a decision Lucas made after coming under attack from civil rights organizations for his portrayal of Jar Jar Binks as a shuffling, simple-minded caricature of a black servant. While Jar Jar Binks will return in *Episode II*, he will be surrounded by characters recognizable as Asian, Hispanic, and Native American.

Production on the Australian leg of the project wrapped on August 25, 2000, at 4:45 p.m., sending the cast and crew back to the States for a few days before proceeding to Italy and London to shoot additional scenes.

Banned from talking to Natalie in Sydney, the Australian press descended on the actress in Los Angeles and New York after her return. What the reporters really wanted to talk about was *Star Wars*; however, since Lucas had asked all the actors to keep mum about the production, the media focused on how the movies had affected her life.

Natalie told a reporter from the *West Australian Newspaper* that she'd been surprised by public reaction to *The Phantom Menace*. She'd expected to be mobbed by *Star Wars* fans wherever she went, but that hadn't happened. "I pretty much have anonymity and it really hasn't changed from before I did *Star Wars*."

Even so, Natalie told the *Sydney Morning Herald* that being recognized by the public makes her very uncomfortable, especially when people stare at her. It is one reason why she is reevaluating her film career. "I'm trying to explore as many things as I can in school and see what I like and not limit myself. I've been acting for ten years, so if I stopped now I would have had a full career."

* * *

When Natalie returned to Harvard in the fall of 2000, she was assigned to the same dormitory. Unlike most of the other students, who'd returned to their parents' homes during the summer months, Natalie had lived out of the country for most of the summer.

She never did anything halfway. When she left the security of her parents' home in the fall of 1999, she did so with the knowledge that she'd probably never return to it, at least not to live with her parents for any extended period.

Even though Natalie had successfully left home, that in itself hardly put her on equal footing with her college peers. When students gathered in the commons area or the dining hall to talk about what they had done over the summer, no one had stories to compare with "Oh, I did a *Star Wars* film!"

Another thing that set Natalie apart was that she now had a bodyguard. The muscular, well-mannered man did not shadow her activities on campus, but whenever she left the campus he was there to keep her out of harm's way.

Having a bodyguard is not unusual in today's society, not since the 1980 assassination of John Lennon by a deranged fan, but what was unusual was Natalie's growing sense of isolation about her career, a feeling symbolized by her use of a bodyguard. Natalie was a public figure, yet she expressed frustration to reporters about the very people who'd made her wealth and celebrity possible. She wanted as little contact with her fans as possible.

If that sounds unkind, it is not meant to be because who can blame Natalie for having a bodyguard or being wary of the motivations of her fans? At issue is her sense of values about her fame. Those values are still developing. Indeed she would be the first to tell you she hasn't yet figured out who she is or wants to be, but the battle lines seem to have been formed along familiar territory.

Natalie's mother was born in America, a country in which personal and political freedoms are derived solely from the power of a free press. Her father was born in Israel, a country in which personal and political freedoms are derived from the might of the military and government control of the press. Since Natalie is a product of both environments, is it any wonder that she sometimes seems to be confused about her obligations as a public figure in a democratic society?

"People are like—'you want your privacy, why would you be in *Star Wars*?'" she told *SAIN Unlimited*, an Australian-based magazine. "I didn't know what it was going to be like. It's hard to get people to understand that too, and you know, if you say you don't want to take a picture with someone, they walk away thinking, 'what a bitch!' And that hurts, too."

When fans stare at Natalie, she stares back at them, thinking that it will make them as uncomfortable as it makes her, but that is rarely the case. If anything, a stare from her is confirmation of the imaginary relationships her fans have with her.

The fact that Natalie is trying to sort that out for herself is one of the endearing qualities that help to define the actress as an adult. Indeed, her friendship with the techno-pop singer Moby is based as much on his political opinions as on his music. When he made an album in 1997 titled *Animal Rights*, it was not a marketing gimmick. He is a vegetarian and an animal rights activist, and he uses his concerts and music to advance those causes. In truth, that's why Natalie was first attracted to him. After she left Austin, she stayed in frequent contact with him, exchanging five-page letters every day for three weeks. After that, they mostly communicated by e-mail.

Shortly before returning to Harvard in the fall of 2000, Natalie did an interview with *Marie Claire* magazine during which she was told that Moby had claimed a romantic relationship with her.

"He did? No, he didn't!" Natalie insisted. "We're going to have a talk, then, because that's not true. Not at all. . . . I love Moby, but it's more intense than a romance. It's a really good friendship. A soul connection."

That was the last interview Natalie gave that year. She didn't do another interview for a long time. For the 2000–2001 school year, she dropped out of public view. There was no reason for her to be doing interviews since she had no projects to promote.

The only notable off-campus attention Natalie received during the school year was as a finalist in *FHM* magazine's 2001 "100 sexiest women in the world" competition. To the embarrassment of her fans, she placed eighty-fourth. That put her ahead of Sandra Bullock, Mariah Carey, and Kate Hudson but far behind the first-place finish of Jennifer Lopez and the third-place finish of her ideological archrival Britney Spears. Natalie's Internet fans took the low ranking pretty hard, as if it were an insult to them as well as to her. The chat rooms and posting boards were ablaze for months with righteous indignation. To some of her fans, she was a battle flag, a symbol of their values, hopes, and aspirations.

Where is Natalie, and what is she doing? Her fans wanted to know.

What she was doing was working hard at Harvard, a university that doesn't offer extra credits for appearing in movies. By the second year there, she had decided to seek a major in psychology, a field of study that put her in line with her biographer. It is not an easy major, but it is one that, once you get into the groove, allows you as much enjoyment as is currently allowed under academic law.

"Many people stay on the lookout for Natalie," said Harvard student Brandon Molina. "I actually do not see her that often, but people always stop and stare [when she passes]. She doesn't seem to be caught up with the fact that she has instant popularity or that people treat her like an object. I am not by any means a close friend or even an acquaintance, just a third-party observer. I would say that she must be put in social scenes that are probably awkward, but I have never seen or heard of her losing her composure."

* * *

Natalie had no sooner left the Harvard campus for the 2001 summer recess than *New York* magazine proclaimed her its "Summer Fun Cover Girl." Among the nine reasons it listed her for that honor was her definition of summer fun in the city: "I think the New York Public Library is so, so amazing. It's literally the coolest place—it's a good shelter from the sun—and it's the most beautiful building. I just went there the other day and it was really, really fun."

Although Natalie had wrapped up her second year at Harvard with little fanfare, she returned to the stage like a bug drawn to a bright light, this time for a role in Mike Nichols's production of Anton Chekhov's masterpiece, *The Seagull*. Costarring with her in the play were Meryl Streep, Kevin Kline, and John Goodman.

For New Yorkers, it was the event of the summer. Held in Delacorte Theater in Central Park, it was presented in an open-air venue free of charge, but there was a catch: you had to have a ticket to see the play, and to receive a ticket you had to line up each morning at the Public Theater office on Lafayette Street. It was first come, first served.

For the actors themselves, it was an opportunity to spread their wings in a *real* drama. Certainly, none of the actors did it for the money involved; the paycheck for each actor amounted to just $646 a week.

A classic for more than one hundred years, *The Seagull* is about a well-known actress, Arkadina (played by Meryl Streep), who deals with questions related to fame, sex, love, and family as her young lover, a famous writer named Trigorin (played by Kevin Kline), falls in love with a young actress named Nina (played by Natalie). The relationship between

164

Arkadina and Trigorin is complicated by the fact that Arkadina's son, Konstantin (played by Philip Seymour Hoffman), is fiercely jealous of Trigorin's success. It was a perfect vehicle for Natalie's talents, not just because its themes of fame, family, and sex were relevant to her own life, but also because Chekhov's style of writing is subtle but deeply psychological. Natalie the quipster did not have to work herself up into an emotional state to play the role—she *was* Nina.

The reviews were mixed , with *USA Today* praising Natalie for the manner in which she managed Nina's metamorphosis into a "prematurely world-weary young woman," and the *New York Times* criticizing her for not showing the "fluidity" required of the character."

* * *

When Natalie returned to Harvard in the fall of 2001, it was to live in a new dormitory with a different level of classmates. She had spent two years in the freshman dorm; now she was in a residence filled with juniors and seniors. The conversation was different, the expectations were different, and the opportunities were different.

Working with Streep, Goodman, and Kline had been an exhilarating experience for Natalie. To her credit, throughout her career she has striven to pit herself against the best actors in the world; never has she taken the easy route to stardom by using sex or controversy. But once she returned to Harvard's intense academic and social pace she switched gears with the unctuous ease of a trucker barreling down an open highway.

For the most part, Harvard students are protective of Natalie, but you get the feeling that their protectiveness is related not so much to her fame as to the fact that she is one of them, a peer who lives in the same adolescent-protected universe. That is all Natalie ever really wanted from her fellow students, that and the right to explore the same academic and social territory.

"Natalie was just another student, more recognizable, and much smaller than I expected, but nothing to worry about, especially because you run into so many famous people going to Harvard, it's like you realize that they are just other kids with different jobs than the rest of us," said student Brandon Renken. "At first you would think of a sense of envy or jealousy, the desire for fame, but the truth is I always wanted to go to Harvard, and here I am. . . . [T]he random [celebrity] sightings just make for good anecdotes to tell friends at home."

By the spring of 2002, as Natalie headed toward the completion of her third year at Harvard, she prepared for the release of *Star Wars: Episode II—Attack Of the Clones* and the filming of the third and final installment in the trilogy. Her days at Harvard were numbered, but for better or worse she would be Queen Amidala for the remainder of her life.

Upon the release of *Attack of the Clones,* Natalie described the film as producer George Lucas's *Titanic.* By that she meant that there was a love story at the heart of the considerable action that has come to characterize a Lucas film. Technically, he was able to do things that were not possible for previous films. For example, he was able to stage a fully digitized fight scene for Yoda, who was 874 years old at the time. The love story was left in the capable hands of Natalie (Padme' Amidala, the post-pubescent queen turned senator) and Hayden Christensen (Akakin Skywalker, destined to morph into Darth Vader, the evil knight of the empire). The highlight of the film is the moment that Anakin and Amidala experience their first kiss, an electric moment that foreshadows the birth of the twins Luke and Leia, the energetic focus of the first *Star Wars* film.

166

In the weeks leading up to the film's heavily publicized May 12, 2002 premiere, Natalie read an essay in the *Harvard Crimson* that made her blood boil. Law student Faisal Chaudhry wrote that the Arab-Israeli violence then taking place was the result of "Israel's racist colonial occupation" of Palestinian territory. Chaudhry described Israeli soldiers as "white" and Palestinians in refugee camps as "brown."

Natalie was beside herself. In uncharacteristic fashion, she wrote a response and sent it to the campus newspaper. In her letter, she said that Chaudhry's comments were a "distortion of fact" since "most Israelis and Palestinians are indistinguishable physically . . . One might have an idea of the physical likeness between Arabs and Israelis by examining this week's *Newsweek* cover on which an 18-year-old female Palestinian suicide bomber and her 17-year-old female Israeli victim could pass for twins." In a display of solidarity with her Jewish heritage, she signed her letter "Natalie Hershlag," the name by which she was known on the Harvard campus.

It is not known what Lucas thought of Natalie's flare-up going into the film's premier—the common belief is that any publicity is good publicity if you have a product to sell—but his thoughts were clearly elsewhere. That same week that Natalie was using her verbal light saber to do battle with an Arab sympathizer, Lucus was meeting with his design team to prep for Episode III of *Star Wars,* scheduled to begin production on June 3, 2003 in Australia.

That summer Natalie endured the endless publicity associated with the film and then returned to her life of relative anonymity as a Harvard student. As a research assistant she worked in the lab of Professor and Dean of Social Sciences Stephen M Kosslyn, who was able to see a connection between her academic persistence and her success as a film actress. "It was very clear when she was a student that she is a very determined person and capable of focused effort over a sustained period," he told the *Harvard Crimson.*

Celebrity law professor Alan M. Dershowitz, who taught Natalie in a seminar called Neuropsychology and the Law, made similar comments: "I didn't know who she was because her name was Natalie Hershlag. It was a few weeks into the semester that I learned she was an actress—but she was a terrific student."

Dershowitz also hired Natalie as a research assistant for a book he was writing. It was during that association that she told him that she wanted to become a psychologist at some point in her life.

"It's all about choice," says Dershowitz. "She has choices and options. She would be a great psychologist, and she's a great actor. She probably influences more people in her acting."

Natalie emerged from her studies in 2003 and was graduated from Harvard University on June 5 with a degree in psychology, turning twenty-two four days later. No sooner had she packed up her belongings at Harvard than she tossed her bags into a cab for a trip to the airport to report for the filming of *Cold Mountain,* in which she played a supporting role to Renee Zellweger, Nicole Kidman and Jude Law. Natalie was in the Civil War film for less than ten minutes, but delivered a memorable performance.

Photofest

Chapter 8

Old Man Oscar Dances with Natalie

By the time Natalie showed up on location to film *Star Wars: Episode III—Revenge of the Sith* she had grown weary of her association with her character of Padme. At that point she had devoted ten years of her life to the fantasy film series. She never expressed regret at doing the series, the first two episodes of which were filmed before she was born, but she had come to the realization, as had film critics, that Lucas, as terrific as he was with action scenes, was not as a writer/director who had a deep understanding of the female psyche. As a result, his female characters always seemed to be lacking in some essential quality.

The opposite was the case with his male characters, most of whom always seem larger-than-life and multi-dimensional, the bearers of an unending stream of character deviations. Actresses oozing with sexuality or intellectual combativeness have never stood in line to work with the celebrated man's man director because they know that his interest is not in developing complicated female roles.

In *Star Wars: Episode III* Natalie's character provides the voice of reason to her fellow senators, while emotionally hampered by the fact that she is secretly married to Anakin Skywalker and constantly struggles with the conflicting demands of political leadership and romantic love. In a speech, she attempts to warn the senators of the conflict inherent in their dreams of glory and their fears of a loss of power. Remarks Padme: "This is how liberty dies—to thunderous applause."

Natalie's favorite part of the film did not involve her. She was especially taken with a fight scene between Hayden Christensen and Ewan

McGregor. Stunt doubles were rejected by the two men who acted out the scene as if it were an intricate dance. Natalie considered herself lucky to be standing on the sidelines as an observer.

Reviews of the film ran the gambit from awful to wonderful. *New York Times* critic A.O. Scott bashed Natalie for not having the "range" to reconcile the conflicting emotions required of her performance, but he gave Lucas credit for trying to lead American films back into the fold of contemporary political engagement: "Taken together, and watched in the order they were made, the films reveal the cyclical nature of history, which seems to repeat itself even as it moves forward. Democracies swell into empires, empires are toppled by revolutions, fathers abandon their sons and sons find their fathers. Movies end. Life goes on."

Critic Roger Ebert takes on Lucas's weakness for dealing with female themes, such as when Natalie's character revels to Anakin that she is pregnant: "To say that George Lucas cannot write a love scene is an understatement; greeting cards have expressed more passion." It was a sentiment to which Natalie could have been forgiven if she had tossed Ebert a knowing nod.

For good or bad, her involvement in the *Star Wars* series was at an end. She appreciated the opportunity it afforded her to do other, more serious films, but she looked forward to bursting lose from the goody-girl franchise. Once production on the film was completed, she threw herself into her most adult role to date—as a stripper in a film titled *Closer.* For some it was as if she had run out of a temple into traffic, barred her breasts—and then let out the equivalent of a Yiddish rebel yell. Free at last, she was free at last!

Natalie celebrated her newfound freedom from Lucasland by reporting to the gritty set of a Mike Nichols film, *Closer.* It is about a stripper named

Alice, portrayed by Natalie, who is betrayed by her lover Dan (Jude Law) in what she considers to be a relationship with a future. Unconcerned about his future with Alice, Dan is more interested in bedding Anna (Julia Roberts). Anna's husband Larry (Clive Owen), upon first meeting Alice, declares her to have "the face of an angel."

The film, based on Patrick Marber's award-winning stage play of the same name, is a witty look at chance encounters and the dangerous fallout associated with love freely given and love bitterly twisted. *Rolling Stone* subsequently described the film as one that "vibrates with eroticism, bruising laughs, and dynamic performances."

Several days into rehearsals it became apparent that the coarse sexually explicit language in the script was bringing blushes to the faces of both Natalie and Julia Roberts. Yet they endured, tossing out the forbidden words as if they were nothing more than giddy schoolgirl chit-chat. Later, when shooting began Natalie showed up with a gift for Julia—a necklace she'd purchased on the Lower East Side in New York. In delicate lettering, the necklace spelled out the word "cunt." Julia good-naturedly responded a few days later with a similar gift for Natalie, a necklace with the words "L'il Cunt."

For Natalie, playing the role of a stripper was a long-awaited opportunity to "come out" as an adult actress. Since childhood, perhaps beginning with her performance in the *Professional,* she had known how to flirt with males of all ages without crossing the line; but with the *Closer* she was given the opportunity to cross the line into a level of dangerous intimacy that previously had been out of bounds for her in films.

Psychologically, strippers are complicated creatures. Most were abused as children. As children they learn to recognize different levels of male eye contact, from disinterested to dangerous. As adults they use those skills to snag would-be predators so that they can manipulate them to their financial advantage. Clearly Natalie had good coaching for her role because not only does she demonstrate the slow, contrived physical moves of a stripper on stage, she personifies the emotional trolling associated with the profession. To research the role, Natalie took pole dancing lessons and visited numerous strip clubs and talked to the women who worked there.

"It's such a complicated power issue," Natalie explained to *Premiere.* "The women seem so fully in control. The men can't talk, their jaws are open, they're not allowed to touch anyone so their hands are on their laps . . . they can really get anything they want out of the guys, basically. But the men are paying for it, so they're ultimately the powerful ones."

Before beginning the film, Natalie had an understanding with director Nichols. They would shoot everything the way it was written, including nudity, but if Natalie did not like the finished product she could veto the nude scenes. Taking off her clothes in front of the director and crew was a major step in Natalie's development as an actress.

She had allowed herself to be emotionally vulnerable in previous films, but never had she exposed herself physically to men and women in a voyeur context. Later, when she viewed the final result she did not feel that the scene was crucial to the film and she asked Nichols to delete it. He did as she requested. They kept their word to each other.

At some level, Nichols must have understood that Natalie used the scene to prove something to herself. It was a huge leap, emotionally, to go from *Star Wars* to dancing nude on a pole, but she felt she needed to do it for herself if no one else. Nichols never complained about the deleted scene. Why would he? The film won two Golden Globes, with Natalie taking home best supporting actress and Clive Owen winning best supporting actor. Both actors were nominated for Academy Awards, but did not win.

After watching the movie for the first time, Natalie matter-of-factly told Nichols, "I'm not awesome yet." Nichols told a writer that it was such a "Natalie thing" to say. She also expressed some embarrassment over dancing with few clothes on in the film, so much so that she emailed ex-professor Dershowitz and asked him not to watch the film.

"It was embarrassing," Dershowitz said, admitting that he'd sneaked a peek.

Not long after finishing work on *Closer* Natalie flew to Israel for a six-month stay in Jerusalem to study Middle East history and culture at Hebrew University. She considered studying in Tel-Aviv, but decided against it because on previous visits to that city she ended up hiding from photographers and she felt that there would be fewer paparazis stalking her in Jerusalem. Asked by writers for the Israeli-published newspaper *Nana* why she wanted to study in Israel she responded: "Abroad you hear and read about many different things regarding the conflict. I wanted to study it more thoroughly. It's not that now I have profound knowledge on the subject, it's just one semester. So, I studied some Arabic, some history of Islam, and Hebrew, of course. It was very interesting. "

Before leaving Israel she played a starring role in Israeli director Amos Gitai's film *Free Zone,* an examination of the ethnic and religious strife common to the Middle East. The film is about an American tourist, played by Natalie, who is searching for her identity (her father is Israeli and her mother is non-Jewish). The lives of the film's three main characters, all women, intersect in a manner that the filmmaker hoped would be interpreted as a plea for harmony in the Middle East.

174

The film itself was overshadowed by an incident that occurred during the filming of a scene next to Jerusalem's Western Wall, one of the holiest places at which Jews can pray. The site is supervised by strictly observant Jews, who segregate male and female worshippers by a barrier perpendicular to the wall. Among Orthodox Jews casual contact between males and females is forbidden.

Police had to be called when worshipers spotting Natalie and Israeli actor Aki Avni hugging and kissing in the scene. Jews charged the couple shouting, "Immoral, immoral!" The actors and film crew were asked to leave. Creating a scene among ultra-Orthodox Jews was the last thing Natalie wanted to do in Israel. In an interview with an American television show, Natalie apologized for the incident, saying that it was a mistake to film the scene at the wall.

Later, just prior to attending the Academy Award ceremonies at which she was nominated for *Closer,* she told *Nana* that although she did not feel that she was like everyone else in Israel she nonetheless felt at home in her father's homeland: "In the U.S. I feel like an Israeli, and here I feel like an American. It's important for me, as an actress, to feel a little bit like a stranger. It gives me an outer perspective on things."

*   *   *

When Natalie received a script for *V for Vendetta* she began reading it the traditional way—silently, maintaining an interior monologue as she searched for her character's lines and their relationship within the story. Then a funny thing happened. Once she began reading aloud she became the character. At that moment she knew that it was a movie that she felt compelled to do. She subsequently admitted "begging" for the role of Evey, a mild-mannered innocent who gets caught up in life-and-death political intrigue through no fault of her own. She pursued the role even though she knew that it would require her to shave her head.

Written by Andy and Larry Wachowski, the brothers who created the mega-successful *Matrix* films, *V for Vendetta* tells the story of a futuristic totalitarian Great Britain, where civil liberties are non-existent and the expectation of the right-wing government is that the purpose of the citizenry is to perpetuate the powers of the wealthy elite. Politically this Great Britain is disturbingly similar to the one envisioned by the right-wing element in present-day America.

Natalie's character Evey becomes part of the underground resistance movement when its leader, "V," a masked vigilante played by Hugo Weaving, rescues her from brutish government agents. She falls in love with him and becomes one of his most devoted disciples. Although the film is based on a comic series published in the early 1980s, when *V for Vendetta* was released in 2006, it was labeled one of the most subversive films since the 1970s.

Not everyone agreed. Sniffed *New York Times* film critic Manohla Dargis: "Inevitable questions and objections have been raised about whether *V for Vendetta* turns a terrorist into a hero, which is precisely what it does do. Predictable, the filmmakers, actors and media savants have floated the familiar formulation that one man's terrorist is another's freedom fighter, as if this actually explained anything about how terror and power (never mind movies) work. The more valid question is how anyone who isn't fourteen or under could possibly mistake a corporate bread-and-circus entertainment like this for something subversive."

Ms. Dargis can perhaps be forgiven for her naiveté. Born in 1961 in New York's affluent Manhattan East Village community, where two-bedroom apartments typically rent for $3,000-plus per month, she is too

176

young to remember the totalitarian flirtations of the 1960s in America—the student killings at Kent State, the beatings of students who opposed the war in Vietnam, the illegal break-ins by government agents, to name a few excesses that took place.

Leave it to Natalie to put it in perspective.

"People are asking, 'Does this movie justify violence?'" said Natalie to a writer for *Vanity Fair*. "I think it takes you to look at terrorism from a new perspective. It puts it in new shoes so that you can see reasons where the methods of terrorism might be justifiable. I think when you make any kind of art you're trying to open a conversation. You are not trying to tell someone what to think."

By signing on for *V for Vendetta*, Natalie displayed an attraction for films with an intellectual core that transcended traditional Hollywood entertainment values. If that involved a dark descent into humanity's baser nature, Natalie was fine with that. Films should entertain, but they also should be relevant to the human condition. It was an attitude that also influenced her next choice of films, Milos Forman's *Goya's Ghosts*. Best known for films such as *One Flew Over the Cuckoo's Nest* and *Amadeus,* Forman wrote and directed *Goya's Ghosts,* a drama set during the Spanish Inquisition. In the film, Natalie plays the part of Ines, the young daughter of a wealthy merchant who is seized by the church and subjected to torture on the grounds that she was seen refusing pork, an indication that she must be Jewish. Also in the film are Javier Bardem, who played a priest named Lotenzo, and Randy Quaid, who played King Carlos IV.

The improbable storyline has it that Spanish artist Francisco Goya becomes caught up in the Spanish Inquisition when the daughter of one of his patrons is imprisoned as a Jewish heretic, setting in motion a series of events involving the chief Inquisitor (Brother Lorenzo) and Ines, the mother of his daughter, Alicia, also played by Natalie. Thrown into the story, ostensibly to sweeten the plot is Napoleon's invasion of Spain, which submits the major players to a nonsensical game of thematic musical chairs.

Reviewers were not kind, but Natalie was usually singled out for praise. Wrote *Variety:* "Portman is a particularly convincing muse for Goya earlier on, then spends much of the later stretch wearing startling, uglifying make-up and doing a good turn as a trembling madwoman."

When Natalie viewed the film she was startled to see that she had done a nude scene. It wasn't in the script and body doubles were never discussed. It simply appeared from nowhere on the screen. As it turned out, Forman decided to spice the film up a bit by using a body double for Natalie in a brief nude scene. Apparently everyone was in on the switch, except Natalie.

*   *   *

Something was happening with Natalie.

Ever since her nude scene in *Closer,* the one that she requested be deleted, Natalie had been obsessing on the subject. Truthfully, the nude scene did contribute to the story's development, but five-foot-three Natalie didn't like the way she looked while selling sex. She wasn't buxom. She wasn't leggy. She was not Playmate of the Month material.

Nudity was all wrong for her in that film because she couldn't sell herself selling sex. She had neither the tawdry face nor the boob-job body for it. After a great deal of thought she concluded that for nudity to be right for her it needed to be part of a normal screen relationship, not a perverse reflection on society's shortcomings or a sidebar commentary about violence against women.

Nudity became Natalie's greatest and most unlikely dilemma.

Hotel Chevalier seemed like the perfect vehicle to overcome that distraction. Written and directed by Wes Anderson, the 13-minute film stars Natalie and Jason Schwartzman as former lovers who reunite in a Paris hotel. She removed her shirt and her pants and frolicked on a hotel bed, displaying her bruised body parts in stylized close-ups and grainy long shots. Just as bruised were her emotions. There was no plot to the story, just two characters trading relationships jabs and occasional heavy breathing, slowly realizing that what life often comes down to are stolen moments that often have no future, only vague possibilities.

"Whatever happens in the end, I don't want to lose you as my friend," Natalie's character says, to which Jason's character responds, "I promise, I will never be your friend . . . no matter what, ever."

Hotel Chevalier was meant to be a stand-alone short film, but it ended up being joined to a continuation of Jason's character as Owen Wilson and Adrien Brody join the narrative as his brothers. The brothers have not spoken in over a year and decide to reunite for the purpose taking a train ride across India in the hope that they will be able to bond again as they had done as children.

Although at times the film seems self-absorbed and pretentious, it received positive critical attention. *Rolling Stone* called it one of the best films of the year. *The New York Times* described the film as "an overstuffed suitcase" and it called *Hotel Chevalier* "a small gem." The later was offered free from the iTunes Store and was downloaded more than 500,000 times, primarily because of Natalie's nude scene. Much to Natalie's chagrin the scene was posted all over the Internet, making her exactly the type of porn-site sensation that she feared. By removing her clothes in an art house film, she assumed she would be spared the Internet voyeur lust that had plagued other actresses. Clearly she underestimated

179

the determination of Internet search-engine junkies who stalked her from the privacy of their own homes and posted and re-posted her images.

On the positive side of the ledger, the film did set her free to do nude scenes—or not do nude scenes—based solely on the merit of the scripts. Amazingly a few minutes of bare-ass exposure sucked the hot air out of the public boiler. In many ways it was a liberating experience, despite constant questions from the press asking for insight into what it "felt like" to be naked in front of the entire world. Invariably she smiled, suggesting with slightly taunting lips that it was for her to know and them to find out.

For her next film, *The Other Boleyn Girl*, a historical drama set in Elizabethan times, Natalie joined forces with co-star Scarlett Johansson. They are the Boleyn sisters, manipulated by their father into flirtatious affairs with King Henry VIII, who already has a wife but seems intrigued by the prospect of seducing the Boleyn sisters. Aside from palace sex, the king is interested in the sisters as providers of a male heir to the throne, a responsibility his current wife has been unable to fulfill. The story depicts Mary, the quiet and innocent sister played by Scarlett, as the king's mistress long before Anne, the bitchy sister played by Natalie, succumbs to his sexual overtures.

Off-screen, the pair gave off odd-couple vibes to the crew. Scarlett is Marilyn Monroe blonde, with lusty, come-hither curves and a sexy voice that often dips into the throaty range. Natalie is Audrey Hepburn, a brunet with a tiny waist and a precise, school-teacher voice that seems to promise with perfect pregnant pauses, "Maybe, maybe not!" What they have in common is Jewish ancestry and size. Despite Scarlett seeming so much taller on the screen than Natalie, both are five-foot-three.

Promoting the film because a problem for Natalie because she did not want it to be viewed as encouraging rivalry between women. "I hate that—

it drives me crazy," she explained to an interviewer for the *Times*. "The truth is, it's hard to find a really great girl, but when you find one, it's the best. The vast majority of my friends are guys, but the ones I talk to about everything are my girls." Asked about an incident in which fashion designer Isaac Mizrahi created a stir when he grabbed Scarlett's breasts at the Golden Globes, she responded with a sisterly nod to her co-star, "Seriously, I would want to grab them. She's got beautiful ones, but, Isaac, that was not so appropriate."

The film never really got off the ground, helped by the odd lack of on-screen chemistry between Natalie and Scarlett. They never once looked like they wanted to consider a nightgown catfight. Quipped critic Jim Emerson, "If Russ Meyer had made 'The Other Boleyn Girl,' Anne and Mary Boleyn would have yanked some hair, scratched some eyeballs, walloped each other in their respective kissers, and the movie would have been all the better for it." By contrast Anne and Mary Boleyn communicated on-screen with knowing nods, hardly the stuff of high drama.

Interviews given at the time indicate that Natalie was not aware of their lack of an on-screen chemistry. She described Scarlett as her best scene partner ever. "I felt that we really had a connection," Natalie told *Empire.* "Between scenes we could just keep it locked, and we'd have this sort of rapport that really gives you a focus while everything around you, like the scenery and lighting, is shifting."

Natalie did what she could to promote the film, dutifully showing up for interviews, but she already was moving on to another project. In the *Brothers*, she stars opposite Tobey Maguire and Jake Gyllenhaal in an emotional drama about a wife and mother who tries to cope with the presumed loss of her military husband in the Middle East by bonding with his younger brother. Problems ensue when the husband returns home—alive. Tortured by his captors he is an emotional wreck who suspects the worst of his wife and brother.

Before shooting began Natalie spoke to Army wives so that she could better understand their lives."Look, if I'd stayed in Israel, I would have probably ended up in the military myself," Natalie told *USA Today*. In Israel military service is compulsory for both men and women. "I'm very obedient, very disciplined. I probably could have done it in that way. But otherwise, I'm kind of scared of all of that world."

Emotionally it was Natalie's most adult role to date. She handled it well, learning instincts for motherhood that even she did not know that she possessed. She remarked to one interviewer that the film had helped her come into her "womanhood." Playing the role of a mother, she admitted, made her start thinking about her own future as a parent.

*   *   *

In between filming *The Other Boleyn Girl* and *Brothers* Natalie began a romantic relationship with a little known recording artist named Devendra Obi Banhart. A native of Houston, Texas he was raised by his mother in Venezuela until they moved to California when he was a teenager. *SPIN* magazine has described his free-association music as "ashram-appropriate guitar strums, trippy-hippie tone poetry," which is a nice way of saying that he is an experimental musician who has little hope of commercial success. Apparently Natalie did not care. She was so taken with Devendra's music, she asked him to donate a track to the album she compiled for iTunes distribution, "Big Change: Songs for FINCA," with the proceeds going to the organization, a non-profit that provides financial services to the world's lowest-income entrepreneurs. Natalie reciprocated by appearing in his "Carmensita" video.

Subsequently they were spotted kissing on the streets of New York and between bites of sushi during dinner at Jewel Bako. The relationship progressed so rapidly that she moved to Malibu in 2008 so that she could be closer to him. For all her flirtations with psychology and experimental research, it was becoming clear that her hormones were attracted to individuals with an artistic bent, especially musicians who danced about the cutting edge of artistic expression. Faced with choices between partners with an intellectual foundation or partners with an artistic foundation she has consistently chosen the later. As with most of her relationships, her infatuation with Devendra was short-lived. They broke up in mid-September 2008. It is not clear why they parted ways, but the breakup coincides with her strenuous training and fasting for her role as a ballerina in *Black Swan*, which was scheduled for startup production in 2009. For more than a year before production began Natalie underwent a strenuous level of ballet training that consumed her days and nights.

In May 2009, Natalie spent $3.2 million for a 4,800 square foot mansion in Los Feliz, an affluent district in Hollywood. The house has four bedrooms and two bathrooms, and has provided solace to a string of celebrities since the 1930s. Natalie appeared resolute in her decision to live permanently in California, but she kept her New York apartment so that she would have a place to stay when she visited the city. Asked why she relocated halfway across the country, she explained that there was more privacy in California. Friends could gather in backyards instead of cafes where the curious were ever ready to send out privacy-invading tweets describing a celebrity's exact location.

Natalie continued to pursue a social life, going out with friends and the occasional romantic possibility, but her focus was on the psychological thriller, *Black Swan*. She'd danced until she was thirteen, recalling that she was pretty good, and she felt that experience would serve her well. To her disappointment she discovered that her ballet skills were mostly the distorted remembrances of an overachieving child.

Once her dance classes for *The Black Swan* began she realized that she had a long way to go to make a convincing impression as a ballerina. Her 8-hour-a-day training schedule with Mary Hahn Bowers, formerly of the New York City Ballet, was so strenuous—swimming a mile a day, doing fifteen minutes of toe exercises (a lot more difficult than it sounds), and undergoing repetitive muscle toning—that she frequently got only five hours of sleep a night. She lost twenty pounds in the process and she was almost constantly in pain, surviving on caffeine and pain medications.

By the time production began in 2009, she and director Darren Aronofsky had lived with the idea of the film for nine years. Even before a script was written, Natalie was attracted to the intellectual core of the film—how an artist can have a narcissistic attraction to herself as an artist while simultaneously feeling repulsion toward herself as a person. It offers a darkly fascinating look at human obsession and it's troubling relationship with good and evil.

Natalie plays the role of Nina, the White Swan chosen for a Lincoln Center production of Tchaikovsky's ballet "Swan Lake." Playing the role of the Black Swan is Nina's competitor, Lily (Mila Kunis), who is everything that Nina is not: confident, determined, bold. One gets the impression that Lily has a sexual persona while Nina, who lives with her demanding mother, is clearly inexperienced in that area. Add to that mix, Vincent Cassel's character, Thomas Leroy, an autocratic personality who dumped his previous prima ballerina and lover Beth MacIntyre (played by Winona Ryder) in order to "reimage" the classic work.

184

The dramatic tension in the film swirls around Nina's troubling interpretation of reality as an all-out battle ensues over creative dominance of the ballet. Observed critic Roger Ebert: "It's traditional in many ballet-based dramas for a summing-up to take place in a bravura third act. 'Black Swan' has a beauty. All of the themes of the music and life, all of the parallels of story and ballet, all of the confusion of reality and dream come together in a grand exhilaration of towering passion. There is really only one place this can take us, and it does."

One of the challenges for Natalie in the film, in addition to the physical demands of the dancing (Natalie suffered a concussion during a fight scene and had to be rushed to a hospital for a CAT scan), was being convincing in a lesbian love scene. Reportedly the script called for hugging and light kissing, but Natalie and Mila conspired to take it to an extreme level. In Natalie's opinion, the steamy sex was one reason for the film's commercial success. "Everyone was so worried about who was going to want to see this movie," Natalie told *Entertainment Weekly*. "I remember them being like, 'How do you get guys to a ballet movie? How do you get girls to a thriller? The answer is a lesbian scene. Everyone wants to see that.'"

Natalie and Mila did not disappoint. The scene, which comes midway through the film, seemed to appear from nowhere, its timing critical for its shock value and for the tempting carrot that it held out for additional sex scenes (there were none).

Added to the physical tension of the dance scenes and the psychological twists and turns of the script was a third off-screen component: Natalie fell in love with her choreographer and male dance partner, the French-born Benjamin Millepied (pronounced Meel-pee-yeh), at thirty-three the principal dancer at the New York City Ballet. Originally hired only to choreograph, he volunteered to be the dancing partner for both Natalie and

Mila, thus unknowingly adding another layer to the emotional complexity of the film. Perhaps adding to her character's complexity, Natalie found herself romantically attracted to one dance partner while simulating sexual attraction to another dance partner. Oddly, Benjamin bears a slight resemblance to Natalie's first leading man, Jean Reno, her co-star in *The Professional.*

In the summer of 2010, Natalie and Benjamin conceived a child, Aleph, who was born on June 14, 2011. For those curious about the origins of the name Aleph, it is the first letter in the Hebrew alphabet. At about the time she started showing, she announced that she was engaged to Benjamin and they were expecting a child.

While obviously pregnant at the 2011 Academy Awards, Natalie accepted her Oscar for Best Actress by paying tribute to Benjamin for giving her the "most important role of my life." The marriage did not take place until August 4, 2012. It was a small, Jewish ceremony held outside in the dark at a private home near Big Sur, California, with about one hundred friends and family members in attendance. Natalie wore an old-fashioned A-line white dress with a hem that almost reached her ankles. Since Natalie is a vegan, guests were served vegan dishes, with sweets imported from Benjamin's native France.

Natalie devoted most of 2011 to her rapidly changing personal life, but during that professional down time she signed on for three film projects that promised to keep her busy in 2013: The filming of two motion pictures, *Knight of Cups* and an untitled movie with Terrence Malick, plus pre-production work on *Thor2* (the first *Thor* was released in 2011 and added little to her stature as an artist, despite the popularity of the film).

The challenge for Natalie will be to balance the tedium of motherhood with the volatility of maintaining an emotionally draining career with the ups and downs of married life, something she has never attempted in the past. As a child and a young adult she was able to protect her family from her success while pursuing even greater success, a balancing act that sometimes required her to put her own interests second to those of her father and mother. The question today is whether she will be able to hold up under the stark reality of being a wife and mother—and at the same time—find satisfaction as an artist.

Photofest

FILMOGRAPHY

THE PROFESSIONAL (1994)

CAST

Natalie Portman
Jean Reno
Gary Oldman
Danny Aiello
Ellen Greene
Frank Senger
Peter Appel
Michael Badalucco

Producer: Luc Besson (Gamont-Les Films Du Dauphin Productions)
Director: Luc Besson
Written by: Luc Besson
Music by: Eric Serra
Rating: R (for scenes of graphic violence and for language)
Running time: 110 minutes

    Natalie plays the role of a 12-year-old, street-savvy girl (Mathilda) who is orphaned when corrupt DEA agents murder her family over a drug deal that has gone bad. Mathilda's life is saved by a hitman (Leon) played by Jean Reno, who lets her into his apartment before the killers can kill her.

    Alone in the world, Mathilda partners with Leon. She offers to clean his apartment and to take care of him if he will kill the DEA agents responsible for the death of her family. Later, she asks Leon to teach her to become a professional killer.

    French director Luc Besson walks a tightrope with this film, not over the violence (and there is plenty) or the suggestions that DEA agents sometimes cross over to the other side (federal prisons are filled with such people), but over the way he handles the relationship between Mathilda and Leon. One step to the left and he falls into pedophilia; one step to the right and he slides into a Disney approach to life. He plays it straight down the middle, offering the debatable view that a man can develop a healthy relationship with a 12-year-old girl that is based on loneliness and alienation, and not sex.

In this, her first film, Natalie gives a flawless performance. Given her overly protected life experiences, it is incredible that she was able to slip so effortlessly into the role of a foul-mouth waif from the wrong side of the tracks who has never known a day of "protection" in her life. It is a tribute to her innate talent that she was able to be totally convincing as a female Huck Finn.

No less challenging was the role handed to Reno. The violence was easy, for all it required was an unblinking stare, but the relationship scenes with Mathilda were filled with potential pratfalls. For the film to work, Reno had to interact with Natalie without ever once offering a glance or inflection that could be interpreted as sexual. Reno accomplishes that by drawing the audience into the despair of his pointless existence, a dark place where love has not shined in a long time, if ever.

Initially misunderstood by critics who were reluctant to acknowledge the existence of organized crime, psycho drug agents and sexless love, *The Professional* has since been recognized as one of the best films of 1994.

DEVELOPING (1995)

CAST

Frances Conroy
Natalie Portman
John De Vries

Producer: Marya Cohn
Director: Marya Cohn
Written by: Marya Cohn
Rating: (not rated)
Running time: 28 minutes

Natalie Portman co-stars in this short film about a single mother who takes some of the toughest punches life has to offer, including breast cancer. Natalie plays the role of her pre-pubescent daughter who must undergo a baptism of fire simply to understand what her mother is going through. This film was never released on videotape, but it can be seen from time to time on cable channels that use it as filler between feature film presentations.

HEAT (1995)

CAST

Natalie Portman
Al Pacino
Robert De Niro
Val Kilmer
John Voight
Tom Sizemore
Ashley Judd
Ted Levine
Diane Venora
Amy Brenneman

Producers: Michael Mann, Art Linson
Director: Michael Mann
Written by: Michael Mann
Music by: Elliot Goldenthal
Rating: R (for violence and language)
Running time: 171 minutes

Natalie Portman is only in a few scenes in this high-energy, crime thriller, but, as always, she milks each scene for all it is worth. She plays the role of Al Pacino's step-daughter, Lauren. Her parents are divorced, and she lives in the household with her mother (Diane Venora) and Pacino. Distraught over her relationship with her deadbeat birth father, she attempts to take her own life. She is discovered in the bathtub by Pacino, who rushes her to the hospital.

Heat is a good guy/bad guy cop drama, to be sure, but the pairing of Pacino, a crusading cop, with master criminal Robert De Niro lets you know right away that this is no ordinary shoot 'em up movie. Pacina and De Niro only meet twice—once in a restaurant, where they spar over a cup of coffee, and at the end of the movie, when the showdown between them occurs—but the psychological tension between the two men is exploited brilliantly throughout the film.

The characters portrayed by Pacino and De Niro are interchangeable in many ways. Both men are obsessed with their jobs and doomed in their efforts to have meaningful relationships outside their work. For each man, winning is the only true gift life has to bestow. Of course, in this instance, winning is not an option for both men.

This is not a psychological thriller (there is simply too much hardware in it to allow it to cross that line) but it comes close thanks primarily to the acting of Pacino and De Niro. Matching them line-for-line in intensity is a supporting cast that rises to the occasion, with each actor treating his or her lines as if they are the most important in the movie. Especially convincing are Ashley Judd and Val Kilmer, a married couple whose marital problems threaten the criminal syndicate of which Kilmer is a member.

MARS ATTACKS! (1996)

CAST

Jack Nicholson
Glenn Close
Annette Bening
Pierce Brosnan
Danny Devito
Natalie Portman
Jim Brown
Martin Short
Sarah Jessica Parker
Michael J. Fox
Rod Steiger
Tom Jones

Producer: Tim Burton and Larry Franco
Director: Tim Burton
Screenplay by: Jonathan Gems

Natalie Portman plays the president's daughter (Taffy) in this wicked satire about a Martian invasion that turns the world on its ear. Not until the end, when she presents the movie's hero with a medal of honor on her deceased parents' behalf, does her dialogue extend past one or two lines in any one scene.

Most of the scenes with Natalie in them have her responding with biting (and sometimes funny) one-liners. Visually, she is almost zombie-like in the way she decorates the White House furniture. When she walks, it is with all the vigor of a zombie on a death mission. Even so, when the movie ends you get the feeling that America will be in good hands with Natalie as its leader.

In dual roles, Jack Nicholson plays both President Dale and a Las Vegas hustler who spends much of the movie promoting plans for a new hotel. Dual roles mean dual wives—Glenn Close as the First Lady and Annette Bening as the hustler's alcoholic wife—but poor Jack never achieves on-screen intimacy with either woman.

This movie has more stars in it than an Academy Awards ceremony, but the characters are so shallow and fleeting it scarcely matters. Rod Steiger plays a psycho general that seems a little too close to the actor himself to ever allow the audience to relax; the lovely Sarah Jessica Parker plays a ditzy fashion reporter who is not far removed from the actress's persona during her visits to the *Late Show with David Letterman*; Pierce Brosnan plays a liberal academic who never seems to be right about anything; Martin Short plays the presidential press secretary with a loathsomeness that is all too familiar to CNN viewers; Jim Brown plays a washed up prize fighter who is trying to salvage his dignity; and Michael J. Fox plays a television news reporter who never gets a break.

From a special effects point of view, the bulbous-headed, animated Martians are a real treat to watch, except for the fact that they kill off the movie's stars every opportunity they get. Clearly, they do not possess the good manners necessary for a take-over of worldwide dimensions.

Director Tim Burton conceived *Mars Attacks* as a spoof on the science fiction movies of the 1950s, but it comes across as more of a spoof on a spoof. The fact that it was released around the same time as the blockbuster film *Independence Day* did nothing to enhance its appeal, primarily because effective satire requires a moderate amount of distance between the target and the missile. *Mars Attacks* was forced to stand eyeball to eyeball with its target—and it was no match.

EVERYONE SAYS I LOVE YOU (1996)

CAST

Natalie Portman
Alan Alda
Woody Allen
Drew Barerymore
Lukas Haas
Goldie Hawn
Natasha Lyonne
Edward Norton
Julia Roberts
Tim Roth

Producer: Robert Greenhut
Director: Woody Allen
Written by: Woody Allen
Rating: R (profanity)
Running time: 101 minutes

Natalie Portman plays the role of Alan Alda's daughter in this situation comedy about a wealthy Upper East Side family whose relationships with each other and those around them fall apart at the least provocation.

What makes it unique is Woody Allen's decision to make the film as a musical of the sort that entertained moviegoers in the 1930s and 1940s. That sounds like a terrible idea, but it actually works, probably because the actors, none of whom are trained singers, all seem in awe that they have been asked to be in a musical.

Alda's screenwife Goldie Hawn, has the best voice of the cast, but that is not saying too much. Natalie only gets a few bars into her one solo before she chokes. That's part of the charm of this film, of course—watching this cast of major-league actors deal with their limitations as singers.

Two of the surprises of this film are Julia Roberts and Drew Barrymore. Roberts is Allen's love interest, while Barrymore is Alda's oldest daughter. Both actresses seem so enamored of their characters that they look positively giddy throughout the film.

Woody Allen is at his best when he ridicules social convention and he takes no prisoners in this film, tackling everything from liberal guilt to romantic love. It is the sort of movie that you don't want to miss, but, once you've seen it, you probably will never want to see it again.

BEAUTIFUL GIRLS (1996)

CAST

Natalie Portman
Matt Dillon
 Lauren Holly
Timothy Hutton
Mira Servino
Uma Thurman
Rosie O'Donnell
Michael Rapaport
Annabeth Gish
Noah Emmerich
Max Perlich
Martha Plimpton

Producer: Cary Woods
Director: Ted Demme
Written by: Scott Rosenberg
Rating: R (for profanity)
Running time: 113 minutes

Natalie Portman plays the role of a precocious 13-year-old who captures the heart of 20-something Timothy Hutton who returns to his hometown for a high-school reunion. Although Hutton's flirtations with Natalie are innocent and never progress beyond the dictates of good taste, they are the high point of the film. At that stage of her career, no one could out-Lolita Natalie and those talents were certainly put to good use here.

Beautiful Girls is basically a remake of the time-proven "reunion" story, though its characters, age-wise at least, come in somewhere between those in *Diner* and *The Big Chill*. Three of the former classmates work as snowplow operators, a fourth is a factory manager, another is a bar owner, and Hutton is a piano player who cannot quite get his career on track. As you would expect in a story about men and women in their late twenties, the dramatic tension (and comedy) revolves about relationships. Who is happy and who is not—that's the stuff of which high school reunions are made.

This is not a great film, but it has its moments.

STAR WARS I: THE PHANTOM MENACE   (1999)

CAST

Natalie Portman
Liam Neeson
Ewan McGregor
Jake Lloyd
Ian McDiarmid
Anthony Daniels
Kenny Baker
Frank Oz
Pernilla August

Producer: Rick McCallum
Director: George Lucas
Written by: George Lucas
Music by: John Williams
Rating: PG
Running time: 133 minutes

Natalie Portman handles dual roles as Queen Amidala, ruler of the planet Naboo, and the queen's handmaiden. As the movie begins, Jedi Master Qui-Gon Jinn (Liam Neeson) and his young apprentice Obi-Wan Kenobi (Ewan McGregor) are sent to Naboo to settle a dispute between the Republic and the renegade Trade Federation.

While the Jedi Knight and his apprentice are on the Trade Federation's flagship, the Federation launches a military attack against Naboo. The Jedi escape from the flagship and make their way to Naboo, where they rescue Queen Amidala and seek refuge on the planet Tatooine. It is at this point that young Anakin Skywalker (Jake Lloyd) enters the picture. As all Star

Wars fans know, the cute Anakin grows up to become the dreaded villain of the universe, Darth Vader.

The first thing you notice when you watch this movie is that it doesn't have much in the way of a plot development and even less character development. That sort of criticism would be disastrous to any other movie, but *Star Wars* is in a class unto itself. *Star Wars* is special because of its special effects, futuristic inventions, and high energy levels. Character development would only be a distraction to the series' true mission.

Watching this film is a little like participating in a high-speed auto race. The story takes you on hairpin turns and white-knuckle accelerations, and then snaps your imagination with exhilarating surges of fantasy. When the final credits roll, the last thing you think about is how the characters' relationships with each other developed.

ANYWHERE BUT HERE (1999)

CAST

Natalie Portman
Susan Sarandon
Bonnie Bedelia
Hart Bochner
Caroline Aaron
Corbin Allred
Eileen Ryan
Heather DeLoach
John Carroll Lynch

Producer: Laurence Mark
Director: Wayne Wang
Written by: Alvin Sargent
Music by: Danny Elfman
Rating: PG-13 (sexual content)
Running time: 114 minutes

Adele August (Susan Sarandon) is a manic, sexually adventuresome mother and wife who leaves her husband in a small Wisconsin town to pursue her dream in Beverly Hills, California. Exactly what that dream is, beyond catapulting her daughter Ann (Natalie Portman) into a career as an actress, becomes muddled as the story progresses.

In recent years, Sarandon has acquired a reputation as a chick-flick queen who portrays women on the prowl for their "true-self power." She plays that role in this case with emotional abandon, but it is Natalie who runs away with the film. She does that by becoming the exact opposite of her mother. Adele reacts with emotion; Ann reacts with wit and intelligence. Ann improvises her life as she goes along; Ann has a plan, the first step of which is to escape the smothering attentions of her mother. Adele is passionate; Ann is calculating. Adele runs away from reality; Ann runs toward it with an open mind.

As the story unwinds, it becomes evident that Adele's search for meaning in life is never going to progress much beyond where it is already. Ann, on the other hand, has reason to hope for a better life.

Natalie has a real talent for drawing the audience into her world while showing a minimum amount of emotion. For that very reason, when she does show emotion, such as breaking down in tears, the effect on the audience is sometimes surprising in its intensity.

Star Wars is the film that made Natalie an international star, but *Anywhere But Here* is the film that established her as a serious actress.

WHERE THE HEART IS (2000)

CAST

Natalie Portman
Ashley Judd
Stockard Channing
Joan Cusack
James Frain
Dylan Bruno
Keith David
Laura House
Sally Field

Producer: Matt Williams
Director: Matt Williams
Written by: Lowell Ganz and Babaloo Mandel

Music by: Mason Daring
Rating: PG-13 (language, sexual situations)

Novalee Nation (Natalie Portman) is a pregnant, 17-year-old Tennessee woman without dreams or prospects who sets out for California with a redneck boyfriend (Dylan Bruno) in a $80 car with a rusted-out floorboard. They make it as far as Sequoyah, Oklahoma, where they stop so that Novalee can go to the restroom in a Wal-Mart. When she returns to the parking lot, she discovers that her boyfriend has abandoned her.

With only a few dollars and no place to go, Novalee homesteads in Wal-Mart, where she secretly eats, sleeps, and bathes in the restroom sink. All that comes to an end when she gives birth to her baby and attracts media attention as the mother of the "Wal-Mart baby." After giving birth, Novalee wakes up in the hospital where she meets Lexie Coop (Ashley Judd), the nurse who cares for her and befriends her for the duration of a roller-coaster ride though the emotional hell of small-town life.

Love, death, betrayal, a kidnapping, a cataclysmic act of God—all move the story along at a disjointed and manic clip that often threatens to out-run the characters. Natalie does an admirable job with Novalee, although Tennesseans might be forgiven if they giggle over her Long Island-hatched Southern accent. The best scenes are those in which she forgets about the accent and allows Novalee to find her own level.

This is a chick flick, to be sure, but it is not without its real-world moments. For that, director Matt Williams can thank Natalie's passion for perfection.

STAR WARS: EPISODE II (2002)

CAST

Natalie Portman
Ewan McGregor
Hayden Christensen
Ian McDiarmid
Pernilla August
Ahmed Best
Anthony Daniels

Samuel L. Jackson
Frank Oz
Andy Secombe
Silas Carson
Oliver Ford Davies
Kenny Baker
Christopher Lee
Jimmy Smits
Rose Byrne

Produced by: George Lucas, Rick McCallum
Directed by: George Lucas
Written by: George Lucas and Jonathan Hales

Queen Amidala matures as a ruler—and as a woman—and forms a romantic relationship with Anakin Skywalker, the slave boy who helped save her kingdom from the Trade Federation. Responding to critics of *The Phantom Menace* who said that Jar Jar Binks was a racist caricature of an African American, director George Lucas added new characters that could readily be identified as Asian, American Indian, and Hispanic.

COLD MOUNTAIN (2003)

CAST

Natalie Portman
Jude Law
Nicole Kidman
Renee Zellweger

Producers: Ron Yerxa, Albert Berger, William Horberg, Sidney Pollack
Director: Anthony Minghella
Written by: Anthony Minghella (screenplay) Charles Frazier (book)

In the final days of the Civil War, a wounded Confederate soldier named Inman (played by Jude Law) deserts and makes a perilous journey home to Cold Mountain, North Carolina to reunite with his would-be sweetheart, Ada (Nicole Kidman). Along the way, he meets a young widow named Sara (Natalie Portman) who is raising an infant child alone. After spending the night with her, he hides not far from the house when Union troops arrive and demand food. Two of the soldiers harass Sara and put her baby out into the cold. When one of the soldiers attempts to rape Sara he is killed, along with a second soldier ,by Inman. Sara kills a third soldier. A second story line parallels Inman's adventures as Ada, a city girl, tries to adjust to country life. Unable to operate the farm she inherited from her father, a character played by Renee Zellweger comes to her rescue and teaches her how to survive on the farm. When Inman finally reaches Cold Mountain, he is almost killed by Ada, who mistakes him for a threat. They reunite and consummate their relationship, only to have tragedy intervene.

CLOSER (2004)

CAST

Natalie Portman
Julia Roberts
Jude Law
Clive Owen

Producers: Cary Brokaw, John Calley, Michael Haley, Mike Nichols
Director: Mike Nichols
Written by: Patrick Marber

Dan (Jude Law) is walking on a London sidewalk when he spots a young woman named Alice (Natalie Portman) who is walking toward him. They make eye contact, share smiles, and she steps into traffic and is hit by a car. She is not badly hurt, but Dan takes her to the hospital, where they get to know each other better. A relationship develops, time passes, and Dan succeeds in getting his first novel published. It is about his relationships with Alice, a New York stripper who has fled to London to escape a bad relationship. While he is at a loft getting his publicity picture taken by a professional photographer named Anna (Julia Roberts), Alice joins him and she also is photographed. As the story unfolds, Dan has an affair with Anna who is married to a man named Larry. He ends up having sex with Alice after he meets her in a strip club. Essentially, the story is about how four people resolve conflicting emotional commitments.

STAR WARS: EPISODE III: REVENGE OF THE SITH (2005)

CAST

Natalie Portman
Hayden Christensen
Ewan McGregor

Producers: George Lucas, Rick McCallum
Director: George Lucas
Written by: George Lucas

This is the episode that sets up the events of Episode IV (the original Star Wars movie). As the story begins, the Clone Wars have ended and the Jedi Knights are scattered across the galaxy. When the sinister Sith Lord Darth Sidious initiates a plot to take control of the galaxy, the fate of Anakin Skywalker becomes uncertain. Anakin decides to convert to the dark side in an effort to save the life of his wife Padme Amidala (Natalie Portman), who is pregnant with their child, who will be named Luke Skywalker. In going to the dark side, Anakin becomes a Sith Lord known as Darth Vader.

V FOR VENDETTA (2005)

CAST

Natalie Portman

Hugo Weaving
Rupert Graves
John Hurt
Stephen Rea

Producers: Grant Hill, Joel Silver, Andy Wachowski, Lana Wachowski,
Charlie Woebcken
Director: James McTeigue
Written by: Andy Wachowski, Lana Wachowski

This story takes place in futuristic Great Britain, which has succumbed
to fascism and a totalitarian government that routinely tortures citizens
who speak out against its policies. The resistance is led by a mask-wearing
patriot who happens upon the government assault of a young, working-
class woman named Evey (Natalie Portman). He rescues her from her
attackers and she joins forces with him. Stephen Rea portrays a detective
who is desperate to capture V before he ignites a revolution. As the two
sides do battle, it is left to Evey to determine who is on the side of right.

GOYA'S GHOSTS (2006)

CAST

Natalie Portman
Javier Bardem
Stellan Skarsgard
Randy Quaid

Producer: Saul Zaentz
Director: Milos Forman
Written by: Milos Forman and Jean-Claude Carriere

This story takes place during the Spanish Inquisition, during which
church officials routinely subjected suspected heretics to torture in order to
persuade them to confess their sins against the church. Natalie's character
Ines, the daughter of a wealthy merchant and muse to painter Francisco

Goya, is caught up in the intrigue when she is seen in public refusing to eat pork, an indication to suspicious priests that she may be Jewish. She is tortured at the hands of a church holy man named Lorenzo (Javier Bardem) who becomes her lover and fathers a daughter, Alicia (also played by Natalie Portman). The lives of Ines, Goya and Lorenzo become hopelessly intertwined and further complicated when Napoleon invades Spain and puts church officials in prison.

HOTEL CHEVALIER (2007)

CAST

Natalie Portman
Jason Schwartzman
Waris Ahluwalia

Producer: Patrice Haddad, Alice Bamford
Director: Wes Anderson
Written by: Wes Anderson

This short film occurs entirely in a Paris hotel room. Jack Whitman (Jason Schwartzman) lies on the bed, ordering room service. The telephone rings. It is a woman (Natalie Portman) who announces that she is at the hotel to visit him. The two have a complicated relationship which becomes apparent as the dialog progresses. This film was packaged as an introduction to the film, *The Darjeeling Limited,* an account of three drug-addicted brothers who meet for a train ride across India to meet with their mother, who has taken the name Sister Patricia. One of the brothers in Jack Whitman, which is why *Hotel Chevalier* was paired with the film, ostensibly to provide insight into his character.

THE OTHER BOLELYN GIRL (2008)

CAST

Natalie Portman
Scarlett Johansson
Eric Bana

Producers: Alison Owen, Mark Cooper
Director: Justin Chadwick
Written by: Peter Morgan (screenplay), Phillippa Gregory (novel)

The rivalry of two beautiful sisters, Anne Boleyn (Natalie Portman) and Mary Boleyn (Scarlett Johansson), for the attentions of King Henry VIII is at the core of this romantic drama that is based on the popular novel. They are introduced to the king at an early age by their uncle because he knows that the king is disappointed in his queen's inability to provide him with an heir. Mary provides him with a daughter and a son, but her sister Anne, the scheming brunet, soon replaces her sister as the king's lover and then sets her sights on ridding the king of his queen.

BROTHERS (2009)

CAST

Natalie Portman
Tobey Maguire
Jake Gyllenhaal

Producer: Michael De Luca, Ryan Kavanaugh, Sigurjon Sighvatsson
Director: Jim Sheridan
Written by: David Benioff, Susanne Bier

Shortly before leaving for a tour of duty in Afghanistan, Marine Captain Sam Cahill (Tobey Maguire) takes in his brother Tommy (Jake Gyllenhaal) after his release from prison on a bank robbery conviction. When Sam's helicopter is shot down and he is presumed dead, his brother takes care of his wife (Natalie Portman) and children. To the shock of everyone he returns from the war and becomes convinced that his wife and his brother have betrayed him by having an affair.

BLACK SWAN (2010)

CAST

Natalie Portman
Mila Kunis
Vincent Cassel

Producers: Scott Franklin, Jerry Fruchtman, Mike Medavoy, Joseph P. Reidy
Director: Darren Aronofsky
Written by: Mark Heyman, Andres Heinz

Nina (Natalie Portman), a ballerina in a New York ballet company, becomes consumed with her role in a production of Tchaikovsky's "Swan Lake." When the artistic director Thomas Leroy (Vincent Cassel) decides to replace his prima ballerina, Nina is his first choice, but she has competition from a new dancer, Lily (Mila Kunis). As the dancers battle it out over who will be the White Swan and who will be the Black Swan, Nina drifts into madness, assisted by her over-protective mother.

NO STRINGS ATTACHED (2010)

CAST

Natalie Portman
Ashton Kutcher
Kevin Kline

Producers: Alie Bell, Jeffrey Clifford, Joe Medjuck, Ivan Reitman
Director: Ivan Reitman

Written by: Elizabeth Meriwether, Michael Samonek (story)

As children, Emma (Natalie Portman) and Adam (Ashton Kutcher) form a brief friendship at summer camp. Fifteen years later she is a nurse and he is a production assistant for a television show. When he discovers that his ex-girlfriend is having an affair with his father (Kevin Kline) he gets drunk and ends up in Emma's apartment. They have romance-free sex, but she is reluctant to enter a romantic relationship, so she argues that they should restrict their activities and ambitions to having sex without commitment. Not satisfied with that arrangement, Adam plots to take the relationship in a more traditional direction.

THOR (2011)

CAST

Natalie Portman
Chris Hemsworth
Anthony Hopkins

Producers: Victoria Alonso, Kevin Feige, Craig Kyle
Director: Kenneth Branagh
Written by: Ashley Miller, Zack Stentz, Don Payne, J Michael Straczynski (story), Mark Protosevich (Story)

Based on the fantasy comic book of the same name, this film tells the story of Thor (played by Chris Hemsworth), a warrior who challenges his brother's claim to the throne of Asgard. To teach his son a lesson, Odin (Anthony Hopkins) banishes Thor to Earth to live among humans, considered a lesser species. He falls in love with a scientist (Natalie Portman) and transforms himself into a defender of humanity, ultimately saving them from destruction when his brother goes on a rampage.

THE THEATER

THE DIARY OF ANNE FRANK (1997-1998)

CAST

Natalie Portman
George Hearn
Linda Lavin
Harris Yulin
Austin Pendleton
Sophie Hayden
Missy Yager
Jessica Walling
Jonathan Kaplan

Written by: Frances Goodrich and Albert Hackett
Adapted by: Wendy Kesselman
Directed by: James Lapine
Costumes by Martin Pakledinaz
Technical supervisor: Gene O'Donovan
Location: Music Box Theater, 230 West 45 Street, New York, New York

Natalie Portman plays Anne Frank in this adaptation of the 1955 Broadway stage production. Both plays, of course, were based on Anne Frank's diary, a record of the two years the Holocaust victim and her family spend hiding from the Nazi in Amsterdam. The book was an international bestseller and was translated into more than 50 languages.

THE SEAGULL (2001)

CAST

Natalie Portman
Kevin Kline

Meryl Streep
Christopher Walken
Philip Seymour Hoffman
John Goodman
Allison Janney

Written by: Anton Chekhov
Directed by: Mike Nichols
Location: Delacorte Theater, Central Park, New York, New York

    Natalie Portman plays Nina in this 100-year-old Anton Chekov classic about a man and his mother who spar over the issues of family, fame, and love. Nina is a would-be actress who comes between the mother and her young lover.

BIBLIOGRAPHY

BOOKS

Cader, Michael, editor-in chief. *2000 People Entertainment Almanac.* New York: Cader Books, 1999, 77-195.

Kopf, Hedda Rosner. *Understanding Anne Frank's The Diary of a Young Girl.* Westport, Conn.: Greenwood Press, 1997, 1-10, 54-59.

Landau, Ronnie S. *The Nazi Holocaust.* Chicago: Ivan R. Dee, 1992, 29-47, 174-180.

Literary Companion Series. *Anne Frank: The Diary of a Young Girl.* San Diego, California: Greenhaven Press, 1998.

Moses, Robert, Alicia Potter, and Beth Rowen, editors. *The 1997 A & E Entertainment Almanac.* New York: Houghton Mifflin, 1996, 36-268.

Pratt, Jane. *Beyond Beauty.* New York: Clarkson Potter Publishers, 1997, 112-117.

Spears, Britney and Lynne. "Britney Spears' Heart to Heart." New York: Three Rivers Press, 2000, 1-48.

Yahil, Leni. *The Holocaust: The Fate of European Jewry, 1932-1945.* New York: Oxford University Press, 1990, 15-27, 90-93, 292-295.

NEWSPAPERS AND MAGAZINES

Addiego, Walter. "Tim Burton's Star-Laden Sci-Fi Spoof Just Goes Poof." *San Francisco Examiner* (December 13, 1996; no page available; www.sfgate.com).

Barth, Brad. "Challenges of the Coming Century." *Syosset Jericho Tribune* (July 2, 1999; no page available).

Bennetts, Leslie. "Through the Stardust." *Vanity Fair* (May 1999; no page available).

Bernstein, Jill. "What a Cool Model to Have." *Premiere* (May 1999; page not available).

Bertinetti, Jeff. "Kidsday Laura Bundy." *Newsday* (August 12, 1992; page 85).

Brantley, Ben. "This Time, Another Anne Confronts Life in the Attic." *The New York Times* (December 5, 1997; no page available; www.nytimes.com).

Bowman, James. "Movie Takes." *American Spectator Online* (www.spectator.org).

Brown, Scott. "Darth Data." *Entertainment Weekly* (March 23, 2001; page 18).

Burr, Ty. "Industrious Light & Magic." *Entertainment Weekly* (May 11, 2001; page 28).

Callan, Jessica. "Stars come out at night for Phantom Menace." *London Telegraph* (July 15, 1999; no page available; www.telegraph.co.uk).

Camp, Todd. "Southern Charm & Despair." *Forth Worth Star-Telegram* (April 28, 2000; page 5).

Canby, Vincent. "A New 'Anne Frank' Still Stuck in the 50s." *The New York Times* (December 21, 1997; no page available; www.nytimes.com).

Chainani, Soman. "Soman's In the (K)now: A Pop Culture Compendium." *Havard* Crimson (April 20, 2001; page not available; www.thecrimson.harvard.edu).

-------------------- "Soman's In the (K)now: A Pop Culture Compedium." *The Harvard Crimson* (April 13, 2001; page not available; www.thecrimson.com).

Cote, Simon. "Heat." *Austin Chronicle* September 22, 1997; no page available).

Corless, Richard. "The Phantom Movie." *Time* (May 17, 1999; no page available; www.tim.com).

Clark, Mike. "Pacino, De Niro spark red-hot 'Heat'." *USA Today* December 1, 1998; no page available; www.usatoday.com).

--------------- "Allen's 'Love' Song Can Carry a Tune." *USA Today* (December 12, 1998; no page available; www.usatoday.com).

Culpepper, Andy. "The Once and Future Queen." *People* (2000; no page available; www.people.aol.com).

Demme, Ted and Ingrid Sischy. "Natalie Portman—Cluttered and Loving It." *Interview* (March 1996; page not available).

Dumenco, Simon. "9 Reasons Why Natalie Portman is Our Summer Fun Cover Girl." *New York Magazine* (June 25, 2001; page not available; www.newyorkmag.com).

Dunn, Jancee. "Britney." *US* (August 1999; page 87-89).

Ebert, Roger. "The Professional." *Chicago Sun-Times* (November 18, 1994; page not available).

--------------- "Anywhere But Here." *Chicago Sun-Times* November 11, 1999; no page available).

--------------- "Star Wars: Episode I—The Phantom Menace." *Chicago Sun-Times* (May 5, 1999; no page available; www.suntimes.com).

--------------- "She Became Perfect in Every Area Except Life." www.rogerebert.com.

-------------- "Where the Heart Is." *Chicago Sun-Times* April 4, 2000; page not available).

Feldberg, Robert. "A Pippi With an Attitude." *Northern New Jersey Record* (May 8, 1992; page 14).

Fine, Marshall. "School Daze." Drdrew.com (1999; page not available).

Fischer, Paul. "Galactic Princess Goes Back to School." *West Australian Newspaper* (August 30, 2000; no page available).

Fitzpatrick, Kevin. "The Queen is Ready." *Star Wars Insider* (January 2000; no page available).

Flamm, Matthew. "Wonder Boy." *Entertainment Weekly* April 12, 2002), pp. 20-27.

Forrest, Emma. "Portman's Progress." *Marie Claire/United Kingdom* (November 2000; no page available).

212

---------------. "Natalie Portman on Britney, Good Deeds and Scarlett Johansson's Breasts." *Times Online* (February 24, 2008).

Freydkin, Donna. "Natalie Portman Transitions into Adult Role in 'Brothers'". *USA Today* (December 3, 2009).

Gleick, Elizabeth. "Natalie Rising." *Harper's Bazaar* (November 1997; no page available).

Graff, Garrett M. "Natalie's Here, There, and Everywhere." *Harvard Crimson* (February 3, 2000; page not available; www.thecrimson.com).

Green, Blake. "Summer Arts Preview." *Newsday* (May 24, 2001; page D-11).

Grove, Lloyd. "Natalie Portman Strikes Back." *Washington Post* (April 19, 2002).

Guthmann, Edward. "In the 'Heat' of Violence." *San Francisco Chronicle* (December 15, 1995; no page available; www.sfgate.com).

---------------------- "It's the Real Portman in 'Anywhere But Here.'" *San Francisco Examiner* (November 12, 1999; no page available).

Hammelburg, Bernard. "A Fresh Look at 'Anne Frank.'" *The New York Times* (November 30, 1997; page 4 AR).

Hartigan, Patti. "Natalie Portman Pays Attention to Her History Lessons." *Boston Globe* (October 26, 1997; page D-8).

Haunss, Kristen. "Homecoming a Blast, as Braves Beat Plainview." *Syosset Jericho Tribune* (October 9, 1998; no page available).

Hauser, Marc D. "Final Club Fowls." *Harvard Crimson* (December 10, 1999: page not available; www.the crimson.com).

Hershlag, Natalie, Ian Hurley and Jonathan Woodward. "A Simple Method to Demonstrate the Enzymatic Production of Hydrogen from Sugar." *Journal of Chemical Education* (October 1998, page 1270).

Hildebrand, John. "Research Winners." *Newsday* (January 12, 1999; page A-7).

Holm, Erik. "She's the Movie Star Next Door." *Newsday* (June 29, 1999; page A-5).

JC. "Sneak Topless Shots Haunt Natalie." *New York Post* (Page Six; date and page not available).

Johnson, Richard, with Paula Froelick. "Natalie's No Real-World Warrior." *New York Post* (March 17, 2000; "Page Six.").

Kempley, Rita. "Beautiful Girls." *Washington Post* (February 9, 1996; page not available).

Jensen, Jeff. "Queen of Heart: Natalie Portman walks off with 'Where the Heart Is.'" *Entertainment Weekly* (April 21, 2000; page 29-33).

Kamp, David. "Love in a Distant Galaxy." *Vanity Fair* (March 2002), pp. 198-253.

Kramer, Mimi. "Encore, Anne Frank." *Vanity Fair* (December 1997); no page available).

Lipsky, David. "The Girl Who Would Be Queen." *Premiere* (June 2002), pp. 57-99.

Loewenstein, Lael. "The Most Beautiful Girl in the World." *Daily Bruin* (1995; no page available).

Maslin, Janet. "When Everyone Sings, Just for the Joy of It." *The New York Times* (December 6, 1996; www.nytimes.com).

---------------- "Of Beauty, in the Ideal and Only Skin Deep." *The New York Times.* (February 9, 1996; www.nytimes.com).

---------------- "The Moral: Be Careful of Aliens." *The New York Times* (December 13, 1996; no page available; www.nytimes.com).

Maxwell, Alison. "Meet Benjamin Millepied, Natalie Portman's Husband-to-be." *USA Today* December 28, 2010).

Michael, David. "In Full Bloom." *SAIN Unlimited* (September 2000; page not available).

McCarthy, Phillip. "A Star is Born and Bred." *Sydney Morning Herald* August 27, 2000; page not available).

McKinley, Jesse. "On Stage and Off." *The New York Times* (February 2, 2001; page not available; www.nytimes.com).

McKenna, Kristen. "Young and Restless." *Los Angeles Times* (February 11, 1996; no page available).

McLean, Craig. "More than Meets the Eye." *The Observer* November 24, 2007).

Morris, Wesley. "All Heart, No Brain." *San Francisco Examiner* (April 28, 2000; no page available).

Nash, Eric P. "The Names Came From Earth." *The New York Times* (January 26, 1997; page not available; www.nytimes.com).

Nathan, Ian. "Teen Queen." *Empire* (December 2000; page 113-117).

Neuman, Maria. "Naturally, Natalie." *Jump* January/February 2001; page 69-70).

Parr, Karen. "Natalie Portman." *Detour* (1996; page not available).

Pertez, Evgenia. "The Seagull Has Landed." *Vanity Fair* July 2001; page 46).

Portman, Jamie. "School Is Where Her Heart Is." *Ottawa Citizen* (April 21, 2000; page not available).

Portman, Natalie. "Thoughts from a Young Actor." *Time* (June 15, 1999; no page available; www.time.com).

-------------------- "In Her Own Words." *Seventeen* (January 1998; page 71-73).

Rainer, Peter. "Grace Land." *New York Magazine* (May 8, 2000; page not available.)

Ryan, James. "Up and Coming." *The New York Times* (February 25, 1996; no page available; www.nytimes.com).

Rea, Steven. "Besson's 'Professional' Receives Rare Praise in His Native France." *Philadelphia Inquirer* (November 20, 1994; page F-2).

Rudolph, Ileane. "Naturally Natalie." *TV Guide* (May 11, 2002), pp. 24-60.

Russo, Tom. "Beautiful Girl: Is Portman the Next Foster?" *Entertainment Weekly* (January 1996; page not available).

Seliger, Mark. "The Girl Can't Help It." *Rolling Stone* (May 25, 2000; page 47-52).

Schaefer, Stephen. "Tough Films at a Render Age: Portman's Professional Debut." *USA Today* (November 14, 1994; page 4-D).

-------------------- "Portman's Not-Quite Nude Scene." *Mr. Showbiz* (November 4, 1999; no page available; www.mrshowbiz.com).

Schickel, Richard. "Slice and Dice." *Time* (December 5, 1994; page not available).

Schneller, Johanna. "Her Brilliant Career." *Premiere* (March 2005).

Sharp, Angela Mildred. "Little Miss Professional." *Venice* (undated).

Sheehan, Henry. "A Parisian in America." *San Jose Mercury News* (November 26, 1994; page 3-D).

Siegel, Ed. "This 'Diary' Doesn't Do Anne Frank Justice." *Boston Globe* (November 5, 1997; page F-1).

Simon, John. "Revisiting Anne Frank." *New York Magazine* (September 8, 1997; no page available).

Sischy, Ingrid. "Natalie: A Star and Friend is Born." *Interview* (February 1995; no page available).

Slone, Carrie. "Portman's Prime Smart. Sweet. Serious." *Mademoiselle* (November 1999; page not available).

Smith, Kyle. "Knights." *People* (June 14, 1999; page 60-65).

Sokolowski, Brenda. "Anywhere But Here." *The Anchorage Press* (November 14-24, 1999; no page available).

Stack, Peter. "This 'Heart' Misses a Beat." *San Francisco Chronicle* (April 28, 2000; no page available).

Stoynoff, Natasha. "Stars Come Out for Premiere of Drama 'Anywhere But Here.'" *Toronto Sun* September 18, 1999; page not available).

Stuart, Jan. "A Formidable Force." *Newsday* (January 21, 2000; page D-6).

Torres, Rebecca L. "Excerpts from a dating diary." *Havard Independent* (date and page not available; www.harvardindependent.com).

Unsigned. "Doctors Debate Ways to Prevent Multiple Births." *Urology World* (April 11, 2001).

----------- "Statistical Profiles of School Districts." New York State Department of Education (www.nsyed.gov/chap655).

----------- "Everyone Says I Love You." *Washington Post* (1999; no page available).

------------ "Beyond Anne Frank." *The New York Times* (May 8, 1998; no page available).

------------- "Sex, food, and pron . . .) *Harvard Independent* (May 3, 2001; page not available; www.harvardindependent.com).

Watson, Albert. "The Private Life of Natalie Portman." *Rolling Stone* June 20, 2002).

Wyatt, Gene. "Guess Who We Spotted at Wal-Mart." *Nashville Tennessean* April 28, 2000; page not available; www.tennessean.com).

Weintraub, Bernard. "A Friendship Founders Over Suit by Woody Allen." *The New York Times* (June 11, 2001; www.nytimes.com).

Wells, Jeff. "The Amazing Ms. Portman." *National Post* (April 22, 2000; page not available).

Williamson, Bruce. "Pretty Baby." *Playboy* March 1978; page 101-105.

215

Willistein, Paul. "Natalie Portman is Set on Being Queen for a Franchise." *Los Angeles Times* (June 2, 199; page 4).

Whipp, Glenn. "Portman's New Role." *San Jose Mercury News* (November 15, 1999; page 3-C).

-------------- "The collegiate queen on fake Ids, curfews and big-screen boff scenes (belch!)." *E! Online* (April 25, 2000; page not available; www.eonline.com).

Wolf, Matt. "Child's Play." *Boston Magazine* (date and page number not available).

Wolk, Josh. "Pop Goes the Teen Boom?" *Entertainment Weekly* (June 8, 2001; 27-35).

Zoglin, Richard. "A Darker Anne Frank." *Time* December 15, 1997; no page available; www.time.com).

TELEVISION AND RADIO

Late Night with Conan O'Brien (December 14, 1994).
Late Show with David Letterman (November 24, 1994).
Late Show with David Letterman (February 1, 1996).
Late Show with David Letterman (November 28, 1996).
Late Show with David Letterman (November 24 1997).
Late Show with David Letterman (May 21, 1999)
Late Show with David Letterman (November 11, 1999).
The Tonight Show with Jay Leno (February 22, 1996).
Oprah Winfrey Show (November 11, 1999).
The Rosie O'Donnell Show (January 9, 1998).
The Dana Alliance (December 1998)
95.8 Capital FM (July 19, 1999).
Good Morning America (February 13, 1996).
The Charlie Rose Show (May 4, 2000).
The Biography Channel: Natalie Portman (2011).

POPULAR WEBSITES

www.natalieportman.com
www.portman-online.com
www.natalie-p.org